THE ATITLAN REFERENCE GUIDE

THE DEFINITIVE ECO-CULTURAL GUIDEBOOK ON LAKE ATITLAN

Richard Morgan Szybist

Adventures in Education, Inc.

Sketches of medicinal plants are by Silvia Caceres de Gonzalez. Historical sketch of Atitlan (1892), the partial facade photo of the church ruin of San Andres and photo of church bell of St. Francis of Assisi are from the private collection of Jose Fernando Mazariegos Anleu.
Other photographs are by Richard Morgan Szybist except those by Samuel R. Morgan, as noted.

Printed in Guatemala, C.A. by Ediciones Papiro, S.A.

ISBN 0-9648706-1-4

First Edition

Published by Adventures in Education, U.S.A.
August 2004

This book can be ordered by internet from the publisher at www.adventurestudy.com.
Signed copies are available directly from the author at: rjmorganjr@adventurestudy.com.

Front cover, main photo is of Lake Atitlan. Other photos are otherwise identified in the text.

Rear cover left margin photos from top to bottom are Church Santiago Atitlan, Curandero fire ceremony, Church of Concepcion, Painting by Felipe Ujpan M., Church of San Antonio Palopo.
Author photo is by Samuel R. Morgan.

Table of Contents

INTRODUCTION

"AT THE WATER" IS THE MEANING OF THE WORD "ATITLAN." IT IS A FUSION OF SIMPLE NAHUATL WORDS THAT BELIES THE COMPLEXITY OF THE ENTITY IT IDENTIFIES.

LAKE ATITLAN IS BOTH A PLACE AND AN EVENT IN MOTION. ITS LIFE INCORPORATES THE VISUALLY STUNNING CHARACTER OF ONE OF NATURE'S MOST AMBITIOUS CREATIONS AND THE EXTRAORDINARILY DIVERSE CULTURAL CHARACTER OF THE HUMAN LIFE THAT THE LAKE HAS DRAWN TO ITS SHORES.

ATITLAN WAS BORN VIOLENTLY, LONG AGO, PROBABLY BEFORE THE EMERGENCE OF MAN HERE. SCIENTISTS STILL DEBATE THE EXACT NATURE OF ITS BIRTH, AN EVENT WHICH CREATED A NEARLY CIRCULAR DEPRESSION OF 11 MILES IN DIAMETER, 95 SQUARE MILES OF AREA, AND OVER 1,000 FEET DEEP. THE CAUSE OF THIS HUGE CAVITY, A CHAIN OF EVENTS WHICH BEGAN WITH AN IMMENSE ERUPTION, PRODUCED A UNIQUE MICROENVIRONMENT THAT HAS BEEN DRAWING WANDERERS TO THE LAKE'S SHORES FOR AT LEAST THOUSANDS OF YEARS. CULTURES HAVE CLASHED TO CONTROL IT. VAGABONDS HAVE BEEN ABSORBED BY IT, LAID DOWN ROOTS, AND QUIT "MOVING ON." TRAVELING NOTABLES HAVE BEEN OVERWHELMED BY ITS BEAUTY AND WRITTEN ABOUT IT IN THE LOFTIEST OF TERMS.

ANY EFFORT TO EMPIRICALLY ORDER THE KALEIDOSCOPE OF ITS ELEMENTS IS ULTIMATELY CHALLENGED BY THE SPIRITUAL AND PHYSICAL IMMENSITY OF THE SUBJECT. THIS WORK MAKES NO SUCH ATTEMPT. WHAT IS OFFERED HERE INSTEAD IS A SUMMARY OF THE LAKE ENVIRONMENT IN TERMS OF ITS PHYSICAL LOCATION AND NATURE, ITS CULTURAL HISTORY, AND ITS CONTEMPORARY POLITICAL AND SOCIOECONOMIC LIFE.

THIS WORK IS AN OUTGROWTH OF MY FASCINATION WITH THE SUBJECT AND A DESIRE TO UNDERSTAND IT AS BEST I CAN. I AM INDEBTED TO OTHERS WHOSE WORKS PROVIDE THE ESSENTIAL INFORMATION FOUND HEREIN. MY SOURCES ARE LISTED AT THE CONCLUSION OF THE TEXT. I AM ALSO INDEBTED TO THOSE WHO HAVE HELPED ME LOCATE SOME OF THESE SOURCES, MOST NOTABLY RICHARD ADAMS AND JOSE FERNANDO MAZARIEGOS ANLEU AND TO MY WIFE, SHARON MORGAN, FOR HER EDITING SUGGESTIONS.

THE INVESTIGATION, INTERPRETATION, AND SYNTHESIS OF THE MATERIAL INCORPORATED IN THIS TEXT HAVE BEEN CHALLENGING AND ENJOYABLE PROCESSES TO ME. THE PURPOSE HAS BEEN TO SERVE OTHERS WHO HAVE THE SAME INTERESTS BUT, PERHAPS, LESS TIME FOR PERSONAL INVESTIGATION.

Richard J. Morgan Szybist
January 2, 2004

GENERAL

Lake Atitlan is located in the Central Highlands of Guatemala, in the department of Solola. Guatemala is the northern-most country of Central America, located just south of Mexico. It also shares borders with Belize on its east and with El Salvador to the south and Honduras to the south-east.

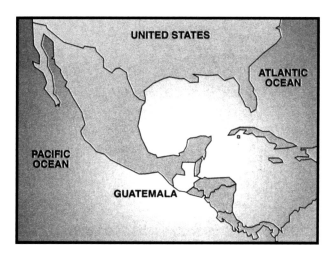

Guatemala is roughly the size of Tennessee. Its coastlines have attractive beaches on both the Caribbean Sea and Pacific Ocean. Its topography incorporates towering mountains and volcanoes, lowland swamps and jungles, temperate plateaus, tropical plains, and river valleys. It has 37 volcanoes, including the highest in Central America (Tajumulco - 4,200 meters).

The country is characterized by an extremely rich biological diversity that includes over a dozen "life zones". These range from desert scrub and humid lowland forests to pin oak and cloud forests. Guatemala claims over 1600 species of vertebrates; several thousand species of plants, (to include over 500 species of orchid); over 200 species of mammals, and nearly 800 species of birds.

Guatemala's climate is essentially constant year-round except for a marked distinction between a rainy season and a dry season. The weather is mostly dry between November and April. The rains begin in May and generally peak in October. Most Guatemalans live at highland elevations where temperatures are generally Spring-like year around. Temperatures vary considerably between regions, primarily as a function of elevation. At some higher levels, temperatures may reach only 55 degrees Fahrenheit during the day. At sea level, the climate can be uncomfortably hot and humid, with temperatures in the upper 90's.

Guatemala has about 12 million people, with the overwhelming majority either Native American or Ladinos in about equal numbers. "Ladino" is a term used to denote those of mixed Spanish and Native American blood, but ethnic identification is muddied by lifestyle and dress. There is also a relatively small coastal population of Black Native American people of Caribbean origin (known as Garifuna), and smaller numbers of Europeans, North Americans, and Asians. Among the indigenous population there are 22 Mayan ethno-linguistic groups. The official language is Spanish.

The dominant religion is Catholicism; practiced in two somewhat distinct styles. Ladino Catholics view their religion much the same as mainstream Catholics throughout the world. In contrast, many Mayan Catholics practice Catholicism in ways that borrow from their pre-Columbian culture. During the Spanish Colonial period, the Church settled into a pragmatic accommodation with indigenous religion. The outcome for many Mayans was a syncretic blend of the two belief systems. This phenomenon is discussed in considerable detail in Appendix 5. In the twentieth century, Catholicism became significantly challenged by Evangelical and Fundamentalist Protestant denominations. Estimates of the statistical balance between Catholicism and Protestantism today vary considerably. Catholicism probably holds about a 10% edge.

Politically, Guatemala is a constitutional democracy, under civilian rule. As elsewhere in Latin America, the military has traditionally played an instrumental role in government. This characteristic has significantly diminished since the late 1980's. At the end of 1996, the Guatemalan government negotiated an end to a 36-year civil war and has initiated an impressive economic and social reconstruction effort with the support of the international banking system, the United Nations, and a variety of individual sponsoring countries and organizations.

Despite the continuing tendency of many "Developed World" critics to judge political developments in Central America by their own standards, Guatemala is a true and dynamic (albeit flawed) experience in popular Democracy. National law provides the right to vote at age 18 without gender, racial, educational, or socioeconomic restrictions. A range of political parties vie for votes in regularly scheduled national and local elections. Since the election of Vinicio Cerezo to the presidency in the 1980's, the country has experienced several peaceful turnovers of administrations, each time with the new leadership from a party other than the one previously in power.

Elections have been monitored by observers from the European Union and the Organization of American States, with the cooperation of the Guatemalan Government. In all cases, elections have been certified as honest. Still, the results have not always pleased many foreigners and educated Guatemalans, as the electorate is largely uneducated and susceptible to Populist rhetoric.

LAKE ATITLAN

Lake Atitlan is one of the three major tourist attractions of Guatemala, sharing this distinction with the ancient Mayan center of Tikal and the classic Spanish colonial city of Antigua. The Lake lies in the Central Highlands of Guatemala, 80 miles west of Guatemala City and 3 hours by car along the Pan American Highway. Just an hour away from the Lake, to the north, is the artisan market city of Chichicastenango. *"Chichi"*, as it is called, is just a step below Atitlan, Antigua, and Tikal in tourist importance. Its indigenous open-stall market place is one of the largest in Latin America.

Atitlan has long been considered by discriminating travelers to be among the most physically beautiful lakes in the world. But, the magic is not just the Lake. It is also in the surrounding volcanoes and escarpments that frame this 130 square kilometer surface of sparkling water. It is in the sun and breeze, playing on the Lake's surface, nudging it into revealing its capriciously changeable character.

It is also in the proud but friendly Mayan people living along its shores, clinging to the essence of their cultural identities while adapting to modern conveniences that fit their pragmatically adjusting view of the Universe. Lake Atitlan's unique natural beauty has been flattered by a host of notable visitors over time. Alexander von Humboldt is the earliest prominent foreigner generally quoted as calling it "the most beautiful lake in the world". This declaration is also commonly attributed to Aldous Huxley, author of *Brave New World*. In his *Beyond the Mexique Bay* (1934), Huxley compares Atitlan to the renown Lake Como in northern Italy, saying that "... Como touches the limits of the permissibly picturesque; but Atitlan is Como with the additional embellishments of several immense volcanoes. It is really too much of a good thing." Probably the most romantic literary description of a first encounter with the Lake was offered by John L. Stephens in the 1854 autobiographical classic, *Incidents of Travel in Central America*. Stephens recounts:

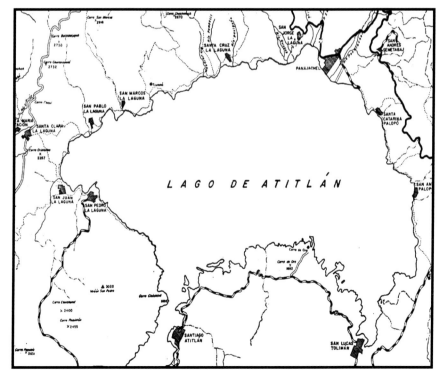

we came out upon the lofty tableland bordering the Lake of Atitan [sic] ... From a height of three or four thousand feet we looked down upon a surface shining like a sheet of molten silver, enclosed by rocks and mountains of every form ... it was the most magnificent spectacle we ever saw ... all the requisites of the grand and beautiful were there; gigantic mountains, a valley of poetic softness, lake, and volcanoes, and from the height on which we stood a waterfall marked A silver line down its sides.

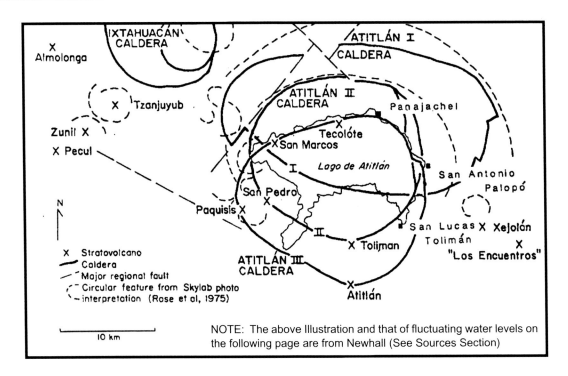

X Stratovolcano
— Caldera
- - Major regional fault
⌐ - Circular feature from Skylab photo
⌐ - interpretation (Rose et al, 1975)

10 km

NOTE: The above Illustration and that of fluctuating water levels on the following page are from Newhall (See Sources Section)

PHYSICAL HISTORY

The most popular general theory of the Lake's origin is that it was formed by a violent volcanic eruption. Just when this happened is the subject of conjecture. Estimates range outward to millions of years ago. An imaginative description of the occurrence has been offered by Jorge Sierra, author of *La Obra Maestra de Vulcano.*

> The earth trembled. The grave and prolonged thunderous sound was supergigantic. The sky, in little time, would turn black. Lizards, snakes and turtles ran to hide. Trees and plants shook with agitation. The largest volcanic eruption of Guatemala, and perhaps America, in the past

million years was about to occur. It would surpass all expectations. Quickly and with surprise, 150 cubic kilometers of magma were expelled upward. It was more than a spectacle. It was a cataclysm, an ugly and deformed monster of fire – like a mythological god. It was a sea of incandescent rocks that exploded to a height of nearly 50 kilometers into the sky... it was violent and with an emission of extraordinarily large rocks.

Atitlan has been studied extensively over time by physical scientists. The Lake basin's physical formation is generally described as a four- part process of stratovolcanic growth, eruption, caldera formation, and continued stratovolcanic growth. Evidently, there were three of these series of events over time associated with Atitlan; creating calderas known respectively as Atitlan I, II, and III. Definitionally, a caldera is a large crater caused by either the collapse of the central part of a volcano or by explosions of extraordinary violence. In the case of Atitlan, the first of these series is estimated to have occurred 14 million years ago, to the north of the extant lake; the second nine million years ago, impacting the north half of the current lake basin; and the third about 85,000 years ago, which produced the Lake as we know it today. This latter cycle actually consisted of a series of eruptions, the most significant of which is known as the *Los Chocoyos* eruption. The net effect was a nearly circular depression of 11 miles in diameter, 95 sq. miles of area, and 3,000 feet deep. It is said that this eruption

scattered volcanic ash as far north as Florida and south to Panama. The depression filled with water and ultimately resulted in the lake that exists today. Atitlan's exact dimensions are somewhat disputed. However, it is described in official literature as about 12 miles long and between 4.4 and 7.5 miles wide. Its total surface area is estimated to be 130 sq. kilometers, with water depths ranging to 340 meters (1,220 feet), with a relatively flat floor. Subsequent to the eruptions, three volcanoes (scientifically classified as stratovolcanoes) "grew" on the southern side of the caldera.

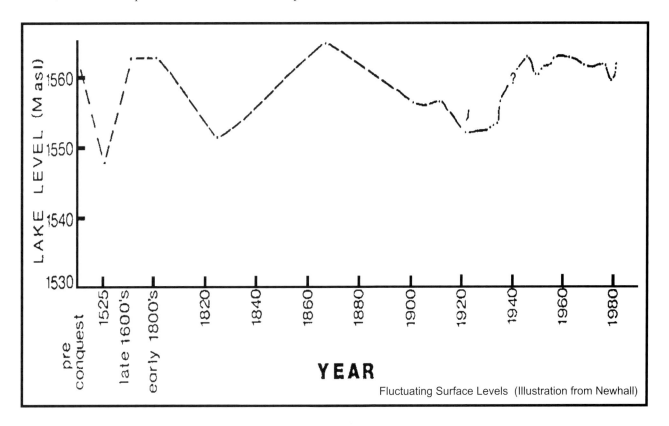

Fluctuating Surface Levels (Illustration from Newhall)

GEOGRAPHY

The Lake Atitlan basin is located in the Pacific watershed of the Sierra Madre Mountains. The lake lies approximately 5,000 ft. above sea level. From this base elevation, land rises dramatically all around the Lake, upward to the 11,600 ft. summit of *Volcano Atitlan*. The terrain is rugged; characterized by slopes of 30 degrees and numerous narrow canyons between 200 – 500 meters deep.

The Lake's surface level fluctuates between one to three meters seasonally, between wet and dry seasons. The Lake also experiences long-term cyclic fluctuations; mostly attributable to rain patterns but, also influenced by earthquakes and other factors. To provide some idea of what can happen, between 1980 and 1998, water level dropped by 10 meters. The 1999 rainy season saw levels rise above many docks and lakeside facilities constructed in the preceding several years. In 2000 it began to drop again.

Increases in levels are mostly due to rainfall and drainage into the Lake. Atitlan is fed by several small rivers. Other contributors to rising levels have been identified by Newhall, et al, (see References section) who noted that the floors and magma reservoirs in large calderas are known to

inflate episodically from injections of new magma. This can also be accompanied by hot spring discharges into the Lake's water body. Explaining drops in surface level, beyond the effect of evaporation, is somewhat more speculative. The Lake has no surface outlets. Newhall et al. concluded earthquake-induced changes in the permeability of volcanic rocks damming the Lake (in the San Lucas area) periodically causes the lowering of levels. Within a month after the 1976 earthquake, Atitlan's level dropped two meters. A Universidad de Valle - MERTW/G study (see References) holds that "underground fissures and seep holes allow water to filter to two rivers draining to the Pacific." Long-term water level cycles have variously been characterized in terms of 30, 60, and 100 year fluctuations. An even longer term view reflects little net change over the course of recorded history. After 2 significant drops in water level in the Spanish Colonial period and another in the 1920's, it has risen again to its current general level.

View of Volcanoes Atitlan and Toliman from the upper rim of the north side of Lake Atitlan.

Guatemala has been bestowed a lion's share of volcanoes. Interestingly, there is disagreement on the quantity. Some sources list 32 or 33. The Guatemala *Club Andina* identifies 37. Whichever of these numbers one settles on, it is an impressive count for a country the size of the state of Tennessee. These volcanoes range in elevation from 1,027 meters above sea level to 4,220 meters. While a few are active, most of them are either extinct or dormant.

The potential attraction of these volcanoes for tourism has barely been tapped. While they are all theoretically accessible to visitors, tour services are not well organized to handle more than a small number of these peaks. Atitlan's volcanoes are a good example. Three fascinating volcanoes flank the Lake's south shore; *Atitlan* (3,537 meters), *Toliman* (3,158 m.), and *San Pedro* (3,020 m.). Each of Atitlan's volcanoes boasts unique features.

San Pedro is one of the most photographed volcanoes in Guatemala. It has a classic cone and stands alone on the lakeshore. The price charged by most agencies for a guided climb of this volcano is about $ 30 per person, unless one makes one's own arrangement in the town of San Pedro La Laguna, where it can be arranged more cheaply. *San Pedro* is the easiest of the three volcanoes to climb and the only one that is normally climbed in one day, up and back. There are daily scheduled climbs. Its crater is the most interesting of the three in that it is steep and obscured by heavy vegetation. This complicates travel to its depths. This crater has long served as a refuge for a variety of endemic and sometimes rarely encountered species of plants and animals.

View of Volcan San Pedro from the top of Volcan Atitlan.

The two taller volcanoes are united at the base and bridged by a saddle. The southernmost and higher of the two, *Atitlan*, is still marginally active. Its last violent eruption was in 1853, but fissures at and near its top still emit steam. On a clear day, *Atitlan* offers spectacular views of the Lake as well as to the Pacific. Only the fittest hikers can complete a climb of either of the higher two in one day. There are no regularly scheduled climbs of these two but, with advance notice, this can be arranged. Agencies normally quote a rate of $ 80 per person and a minimum of two people for such climbs. *Atitlan* is the only one of the three Lake volcanoes essentially bare of vegetation at the top. Its twin to the north, *Toliman*, bears the distinction of having two craters, one at 3,134 meters elevation and the other at 3,158 meters. *Toliman*, like *San Pedro*, is inactive. Its upper slopes are home to some scarce species of birds to include the rare Horned Guan, which also lives on the upper slopes of *Atitlan*.

Another notable terrain feature, *Cerro de Oro* (Hill of Gold), located at the northern foot of *Volcan Toliman*, is scientifically classified as a parasitic andesitic dome of that volcano. It can be readily climbed in a few hours. However, it is hardly offered as a climb by travel agencies. *Aventuras en Educacion, S.A., at Los Encuentros Posada y Centro Cultural* in Panajachel is generally the most convenient source to arrange hikes of *Cerro de Oro* and the two higher volcanoes of the lake.

CLIMATE

The lakeside region is semi-tropical, with the two distinct seasons already mentioned.

Temperatures generally range between the 80's (degrees Fahrenheit) in the afternoon to the 50's at night, year-round. Afternoon temperatures are generally considerably higher in the dry season than the rainy season.

According to Newhall, the Lake's year-round average surface water temperature is about 72 degrees Fahrenheit; averaging 74 degrees between June–August and 70 degrees in Jan–Feb. Water temperature decreases with depth till 60-100 feet, and then remains constant at about 67 degrees F. from that depth to the bottom, year-round.

A unique feature of the climate is a phenomenon known as the *Xocomil* (In Kaqchickel language, "The wind that carries away sin.") This is caused by the encounter of warm Pacific coast winds with colder air from the north, characteristically in late mornings, causing turbulence at the Lake's surface.

FLORA & FAUNA

Wild birds found in the region include native and migratory species. The Lake is the only place in the world where the Atitlan Grebe has been found. This flightless bird (also known as El Pato Zambullidor and, locally, as Pato "POC") is at the brink of extinction. Reported sitings are somewhat confused by the seasonal presence of a similar bird, the migratory Pied-billed Grebe.

Another rare bird associated with the Lake, and one which I have seen, is the rare Horned Guan. This turkey-sized bird has been hunted to near extinction and, today, only survives at the summits of high volcanos in southern Mexico and northern Guatemala. My sighting was near the summit of *Volcan Tolima*n. Other birds spotted on the slopes of *Toliman* on the same occasion were the Fulvous Owl, the Singing Quail, and the Buffy-fronted Wood Partridge. Commonly seen migratory ducks here include the American Widgeon and the Ruddy Duck. The area is also populated by woodpeckers and a variety of wild pigeons and other birds. Sightings in my own garden include the Southern House Wren, the Clay Colored Robin, Baltimore Oriole, Blue-Gray Tanager, Rufous Collared Sparrow, Brown Capped Vireo, Little Hermit Hummingbird, Yellow Warbler, White-bellied Emerald Hummingbird, Golden-fronted Woodpecker, Chestnut-sided Shrike Vireo, and the Melodious Blackbird.

Lake sealife includes three small native types of fish, of which the *mojarra* is the largest, and the Black Bass, which was introduced in 1940's. Crayfish and crabs are also found along the shoreline in some areas.

Ecologically, a water reed called *tul* is the most important aquatic plant of the Lake. It serves to improve the quality of the lake by trapping sediments suspended in the water; aids in detoxifying the water by filtering out harmful chemicals; stabilizes the shoreline from the erosive effects of strong winds and waves; and provides protection and nesting for the survival and reproduction of various animal species (crabs, fish, birds). It also serves a traditionally important economic purpose; artisans harvest it to use as material to weave mats, hats, baskets, and other goods for themselves and for sale. Now, as the lakeside population increases and becomes increasingly focused on tourism and recreation as key

activities, *tul* is being removed by property owners to build docks and create beaches. These traditional and modern developmental activities all serve useful purposes. The challenge is to moderate them to permit the Lake to survive as a relatively clean and attractive habitat for humans as well as plants and wildlife.

Natural vegetation around the lakeside is mostly pine and chaparral, with grasses and reeds along the shoreline. Castilian cane is found in rocky outcrops. Large oak, cedar and pine grow naturally at higher elevations. Dense forest is generally found where steep rocky slopes and natural drainage do not favor farming. The volcanic heights host cloud forests that, in the case of two of the three lakeside volcanos, extend upward to and into the craters. Other native trees include the Avocado, Matasano, Kapok, Wild Fig, Acacia, "Chichicaste" and "Jiote". Epiphytes (e.g., orchids, ferns) live on trees. Cacti, including agave, maguey, nopal and pitihaya cacti, live among the trees lending, respectively, both tropical and desert accents to the plant life. Coffee plants and their shade trees (most commonly *gravilea*), while not native, contribute to the forests. Coffee was introduced to the area in the nineteenth century. The Arabica bean coffee produced by these trees is among the best in the World. A comparison of Landsat TM images in 1986 and 1996 reflect an increase in total woodland over this period due to the conversion of both corn fields and natural woods to coffee planting. It is a fragile trend. Market price fluctuations affect decisions on coffee production.

Native forest animals include deer, fox, squirrels, armadillos, opossums, bats, and monkeys, and other small mammals. Some of these are rare in their natural habitat.

CULTURAL HISTORY

As already noted, "Atitlan" is a combination of Nahuatl words meaning "at the water (i.e., lake.)" Nahuatl is a Mexican language and its use for the Lake's name is testimony to the historical pervasiveness of Mexican influence in the Guatemalan Highlands. Archeological excavations have uncovered ruins of lakeside communities at Atitlan extending back to the Middle Pre-classic period (1000 – 600 B.C.), about the time that the Mayan civilization generally began to emerge.

Mayan civilization evolved out of cultural contact between expansive Mexican peoples and sedentary populations of what is, today, Guatemala, Belize, and parts of Honduras and El Salvador. Mayan society was more decentralized than the societies of the Aztecs and Incas. Powerful city states politically dominated outlying regions and often warred on one another. At its most sophisticated stage, the network of significant centers consisted of more than 20 interconnected cultural communities. Some groups outside of this network were able to maintain relative independence. Mayan society was (and remains) characteristically sedentary and agrarian.

At its peak and in its most advanced centers, the Mayan civilization became distinguished by the development of mathematics, astronomy, precise calendars, and the construction of elaborate ceremonial temples and columns. Over time, Mayan civilization in Guatemala has devolved into 22 linguistically distinct but otherwise culturally related indigenous groups.

Initially, Mayan civilization developed most rapidly along the Pacific coast and in the Guatemalan Highlands. The most notable center was Kaminaljuyu, on the site of contemporary Guatemala City. By the first century, A.D., the inhabitants of Kaminaljuyu enjoyed a culture distinguished by sophisticated fine arts (painting and ceramics), architecture, astronomy, and writing. By 150 A.D., however, Kaminaljuyu (and the Highlands in general) were in decline and lowland Mayan cities, mostly in the north, became the centers of Mayan progress. The dynamics of the decline of Kaminaljuyu are not clear, although Mexican influences are commonly blamed for the general decline in the Highlands. Interestingly, advances in the Northern Lowlands in the same timeframe are commonly attributed to Olmec influences from Mexico and trade ties with Teotihuacan.

It appears that a significant Mexican intrusion into the Highlands took place around 400 A.D. Forces from Teotihuacan annihilated existing elites in areas of penetration, while leaving the peasantry intact to serve as spoils of war. The conquerors rebuilt Kaminaljuyu in the style of Teotihuacan.

After 900, A.D., the Classic lowland Mayan civilization declined rapidly. Centers like Tikal were abandoned and the populace scattered to other areas. In this general timeframe, the Highlands experienced another major invasion by Toltec groups . The Atitlan Lake region was invaded by the Tz'utujils and Kaqchikels, The extant ruling class was eliminated and commoners were subjugated by the invaders who installed their own feudal hierarchies. Bloods and cultural traits of the inhabitants and conquerors mixed, generating the characters of the Tz'utujil and Kaqchikel peoples of today.

What brought the conquerors to this region? According to the *Annals of the Cakchiquels*, these two groups and the Quiche were three of seven migrating tribes that found their way to the Toltec capital of Tula. The ruler of Tula directed them to move on further southward and granted them legitimacy as colonizers under Toltec sponsorship. There is no dependable chronological history to describe the sequence or the dynamics of this migration. Existing documents and archeological evidence suggest that the Tz'utujils were the first to arrive in the Atitlan region. They established their capital at a place they named Chuitinamit, across the bay from modern-day Santiago Atitlan. Here, they built a walled fortress that acquired the form of an acropolis, complete with plazas, temples, and an administrative complex. The Kaqchikels built a similar capital at a place called Iximche, near modern-day Tecpan. The Quiche settled further north near what is now Santa Cruz del Quiche.

The Tz'utujils quickly extended their domain south to the Pacific coast and north beyond Lake Atitlan, to include the area around Solola. However, the Kaqchikels also expanded their interests. Moving southward, they reached the northern shore of Lake Atitlan. According to the *Annals*, the Tz'utujils agreed to divide the Lake basin peacefully with their competitors and the relationship was sealed with an exchange of women, a matter most important to the Kaqchikel warriors who were badly in need of wives at the time. The power balance between the Tz'utujils, the Kaqchikels, and the Quiches alternated considerably in the Guatemalan Highlands and along the coastal piedmont throughout the Pre-Conquest period. For most of this time, the Quiche dominated and, for awhile, they extended hegemony over the other two groups. Quiche power peaked at the end of the fourteenth century. Meanwhile, alliances between the three shifted back and forth and considerable warfare took place.

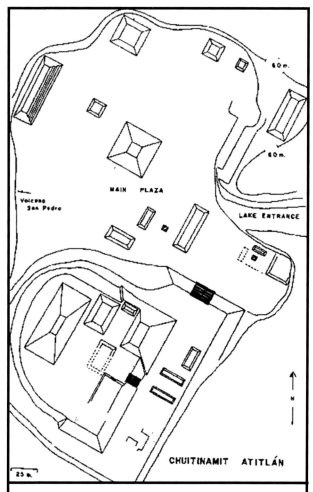

Sketch of the ancient Tz'utujil capital of Chiya', across the lagoon from Santiago Atitlan. This location, at the base of Volcan San Pedro, is a hill knob named Chuitinamit by the Tz'utujils. Chiya' has been classified as an acropolis of the Early Postclassic Period (A.D. 1000-1200).

Depicted in the main plaza area are the remains of a large central pyramid surrounded by square and other rectangular structures. The southern group of structures is on higher terrain and includes another pyramid. This sketch, from John Fox who surveyed Chiya in 1972, is taken from Orellana (See Sources Section).

Intermarriage between royalties continued to be an important means of cementing alliances.

Internal warfare erupted among the Tz'utujils at the beginning of the sixteenth century, following a 20-year period of peace between them and the Kaqchikels. The Kaqchikels intervened on one of the warring sides. After the revolt ended, fighting again broke out between the two peoples. The two were at odds when the Spanish conquistador Alvarado arrived in 1524. At that time, the Tz'utujils controlled most of the Lakeshore, except the area between Panajachel and San Antonio Palopo. Alvarado sent messengers to both the Tz'utujils and Kaqchikels urging them to accept Spanish rule. The Kaqchikels accepted. The Tz'utujils killed the messengers. The Kaqchikels joined the Spanish to subdue the Tz'utujils. Later, the Kaqchikels revolted against the Spaniards, and Alvarado recruited Tz'utujil warriors to defeat the Kaqchikels.

The Spaniards, largely through the efforts of Franciscan missionaries, concentrated both Atitlan peoples in communities to facilitate socialization and control. Ten communities resulted. Interestingly, the territorial division between the two Mayan groups generally followed what had been first agreed upon between the two in the thirteenth century. The Tz'utujils were primarily concentrated in the place which became known as Santiago de Atitlan. Secondary communities included San Lucas, San Pedro and San Juan. The Kaqchikels were concentrated at Panajachel, San Marcos, Santa Cruz, Sta. Catarina, San Antonio and San Pablo.

The passage of time has muddied the details of common roots as well as the developmental enmity between these two proud peoples. The modern-day segregation between them has developed soft edges and veins of interpenetration. Today, again, they share the common challenge of accommodating their shared culture with the cultures of others that compete for control in the Lake Basin. Fortunately, it is a peaceful competition that contributes color to the cultural mosaic of the Lake's population.

CONTEMPORARY LOCAL SOCIETY

Today, most of the population around Lake Atitlan is still Kaqchikel and Tz'utujil with smaller percentages of Ladinos and foreign ex-patriates (mostly North American and European.)

It is tempting but dangerous to generalize about the values and beliefs of the modern Atitlan Maya. Outwardly, the lifestyle appears anachronistic. The reason is twofold. Physically, Lake Atitlan is relatively isolated from the mainstream of change produced by mass communication and the world economic market. This has afforded the indigenous communities the opportunities to accept new things in small bites and ingest them in an evolutionary rather than revolutionary way. At the same time, traditional cultural identity and pride are strong. Thus, relative isolation has allowed the Mayans here to adhere to their identity while slowly modernizing their ways of life. Some communities, most notably Panajachel, Santiago, and San Pedro, are frequented by foreigners in considerable numbers. The contact influences both sides. Other communities like Tzununa see few outsiders.

Mayan Children of Atitlan

Courtesy of Samuel R. Morgan

Mayan Youth of Atitlan

Courtesy of Samuel R. Morgan

Elders of Atitlan
Courtesy of Samuel R. Morgan

The Atitlan Mayans

Courtesy of Samuel R. Morgan

Most indigenous women and many of the children, continue to dress in costumes that extend back to the Pre-Conquest period. There is a notable change with the newer generations which increasingly adopt the clothing of mass world culture. Many older men continue to cling stubbornly to traditional dress. Some communities are more traditional than others. For instance, in San Antonio, many young men continue to wear their traditional clothing on a daily basis.

Mayan women washing clothes lakeside at San Antonio Palopo.

Among the older generations, adherence to tradition does not imply a rejection of modern technology. The Mayan people are pragmatic in evaluating new ideas and gadgets that have penetrated their culture. Things that improve comfort, health and economic productivity are absorbed, to the extent they can be afforded. Meanwhile, mass communication and schoolhouse education are beginning to significantly modify the worldview of the young. In recent decades, the influence of Protestant evangelism has also impacted on traditional beliefs.

Twelve communities are generally characterized as being lakeside. The most important are Panajachel, Santiago Atitlan, San Lucas Toliman, and San Pedro La Laguna. A few miles from the Lake is Solola, capital of the Guatemalan department (state) in which the Lake is located.

There is considerable variety in color, patterns, and figure detail in the traditional dress of Atitlan Mayan women. Distinctions of these kinds between communities, and standardization within a given community, serve to identify one's community of origin. This is much less the case with men in most communities. These distinctions are rooted in pre-Columbian cultural dynamics and are influenced by climactic differences between elevations. It appears that, before the Spanish Conquest, there was some sharing of local styles between groups. The Spaniards formalized and mandated the observance of the differences as a population control mechanism. Patterns, colors, and decorative detail bear coded meanings.

Basic pre-Columbian styles for women incorporate a blouse (knowm as a *huipil*) and wraparound, ankle-length skirt (called an *enredo*, *refajo*, or *corte*). Sometimes these are accompanied by shawls (*perrajes*). Traditional men's clothing – especially ceremonial wear - is heavily influenced by Conquest-period European styles. Traditionally, men wear long-sleeved shirts with long baggy short pants (*calzones*) or, less commonly, short woolen wraps that approximate skirts. A sash (*faja*) generally accompanies the costume, bound at the waist. At higher altitudes, men wear a woolen cloak (*capisayo*) or a short tailored jacket (*saco*). Head bands or turbans (*Tzutes*) are sometimes worn, mostly by women. Men most commonly wear a "cowboy" style, full brim hat. Other styles of men's headcover are largely restricted to ceremonial dress. Traditional sandals (*caites*) are increasingly being replaced by Western style footwear.

The Hernandez family in San Juan La Laguna.

Costumes of some communities are much more ornate than others. Patterns are commonly formed from contrasting panels and stripes and incorporate colorful embroidery with animal, plant, geometric and human shapes. People of poorer communities and laborers in general wear clothing of simpler design. Folkways and dress distinctions from the Spanish colonial period are disappearing. Pick-up trucks increasingly ply new and improved roads which exist between many of the communities. People exchange goods and ideas much more than in the past. With the coming of foreign modernizing influence, men have become less likely than women to adhere to the traditional dress. However, around the Lake, traditional costumes are much more common among native peoples than in many other parts of Guatemala.

The most uniform clothing item within a community is the woman's *huipil*. While "modern" indigenous women are increasingly substituting decorative *blusas* (blouses) of lighter weight than the *huipil*, these retain a harmonious appearance with the overall costume. Considerable variation is seen in color and patterns of the *corte*. Still, the general adherence to traditional dress remains strong.

A gathering of housewives in Panajachel preparing a special feast day meal during the town's annual Feria.

RELIGION

The Spaniards quickly followed-up their conquest of the Mayans with a mandated, highly structured program of religious conversion to Christianity. This program forced Mayan religion underground but did not destroy it. The relative influence of the pre-Christian belief system varies considerably from community to community, and among families within a given community. Catholicism, as elsewhere in Guatemala, is being aggressively challenged by more recent evangelical Christian faiths.

A unique feature of the religious syncretism which has evolved among Mayan Catholics is the system of the *cofradia*. The original *cofradias* were created in Europe in the Middle Age. The organizational concept was "sold" to the Mayans by the missionaries in the immediate post-Conquest period. The *cofradias* were lay brotherhoods invested with the responsibility and trust for much of a church's well-being . They were organized to carry out cult activities and church maintenance functions, as well as to lend a degree of indigenous impowerment within the structure of the parish community. The importance of the *cofradias* around Atitlan peaked between the mid-19th to mid-20th century because of the scarcity of priests in the region (See Appendix 7). Involvement in *cofradias* has waned significantly over time, but activities organized by the *cofradias* in Catholic parishes continue to play an important role in religious celebrations around the Lake.

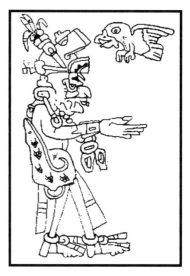

Much of what we know of the Mayan people that settled in the Central Highlands of Guatemala comes from the Popol Wuh, which can be loosely called the Quiche Mayan book of Genesis. This book describes the Creators' experimentations with three versions of man, done successively with mud, wood, and corn dough. The above drawing from the Mayan Codex Peresianus depicts the stage of this drama in which Quel, the parrot, is giving the idea of using corn for man to one of the Creators.

The water color on the right by Rene Dionisio depicts the three versions of man, with the spirit of the Creator, at the right end of the composition, looking on. The original work is on display at Los Encuentros Posada y Centro Cultural in Panajachel.

While the men in these brotherhoods hold the key leadership positions, the prestige of these offices extend to their wives. Husband and wife contribute heavily from their personal resources to lend meaning to these celebrations. Catholic parishes often have multiple *cofradias*. Panajachel, for instance, has five, each dedicated to the veneration of a different religious figure. In these cases, there is a hierarchy of importance among these with the one named in honor of the community parish's patron saint being the most important. In the case of Panajachel, it is the Cofradia of San Francisco. The *cofrade* (chief official) of this lead cofradia has the responsibility of coordinating the collaboration of all five groups for the celebration of St. Francis. The indigenous influence in the Catholic Church is manifested in the setting as well as the ritual the figures are often dressed in native costumes. The wives of the cofradia officers are often the tailors of these outfits. Historically, and aside from its religious function of focusing devotion to sainted persona, the *cofradia* has served as a mechanism for the Church to obtain tribute (taxes, services, goods). Today, the *cofradia* sometimes clashes with modernizing influences of the Church. It's operational role is more to help Mayans retain their traditional identities and sense of connection to Christianity . It is an institution that coexists with Catholicism, but out of the direct control of the Catholic clergy.

In the colonial period through the mid-20th century, *cofradia* membership was a pervasive element of indigenous community life. The classic hierarchy of the organization provides for membership of just about everyone, at some level, and everyone was, at least nominally, Catholic. The position of *cofrade* was traditionally if not legally woven into the civilian bureaucratic structure. Today, membership in *cofradias*

These photos are from the Cofradia of San Francisco, affiliated with the Church of St Francis in Panajachel. Above are the cofrade of the society, Juan Queche Lopez, (as of the Feast of San Francisco in 2003) and his wife.
The statues to the rear, of St Francis and others, are maintained at the cofradia's chapel. They are temporarily moved to the church on special occasions.

is small. In a Sep'03 interview I had with the *cofrade* of the *Cofradia de San Francisco,* he estimated that the aggregate membership of all five of the Panajachel *cofradias* was approximately 50 men.

The wane in the influence of the cofradia can be attributed to a number of factors to include the divestiture of the church's legal status as an official institution by the government and the emergence of competing alternatives to membership in a *cofradia,*

St. Francis dressed in a Mayan costume.

both inside and apart from Catholicism. The emergence of the organization called Catholic Action, within the Church, provided a mode for lay Catholics to be active within their parishes without being bound by the strictures, beliefs, and traditional responsibilities of the *cofradia.* Evangelical Protestantism also drew many away from Catholicism. Apart from religious alternatives, military service became an alternative to civil service as well as service within the cofradia structure. A general weakening of commitment to religious participation, perhaps attributable to the influence of outside contemporary culture, along with the heavy economic expense associated with leadership positions within the *cofradia* structure also began to discourage participation. In his book *Panajachel: A Guatemalan Town in Thirty-Year Perspective,* Hinshaw identifies the refusal of two local men, in the 1940's, to serve in the capacity of *cofrade* as the beginning of the decline in the traditional power of the cofradia of elders and the weakening of the system itself.

The practice of traditional Mayan beliefs is strongest in the smaller more insulated communities

Maria Can Sahon is a Mayan curandera who lives in Panajachel. She conducts individual and group ceremonies that incorporate Christian and pre-Columbian Mayan beliefs and symbolism. She does open-air ceremonies around the lakeside and at shrines in her home.

of the Lake. In some places, Mayan high priests still serve as spiritual guides to people in accordance with tradition. They perform rituals and ceremonies associated with birth, marriage, and death.

Faith healing is more ingrained in the belief systems of the Mayans than among the Ladino population at large. *Curanderos* (healers) are men and women credited with supernatural powers who treat the full spectrum of medical problems, although some specialize in certain maladies. *Curanderos* explain their powers in a variety of ways. Some explanations are rooted in ancient beliefs. Others are fitted into the context of Christianity. In the latter case, the power is characterized as a gift of God to serve man. To some extent, the enduring reliance of Mayans on *curanderos* is driven by an economic imperative. Modern medicine is beyond the financial reach of many indigenous people who live at a subsistence level. *Curanderos* are flexible in their charges and types of payment they are willing to receive for their services.

Folklore reflects the belief systems of the native lake dwellers and much of it is considered by them to be credible oral history. It sometimes relates to beliefs outside the realm of what those from other cultures would consider religious. Probably the most popular local folk tale theme is that of the origin of the wind called "*Xocomil*." This is "the wind that carries away sin." One version holds that its origin is in a tragic love affair between a Kaqchikel prince and a Tz'utujil princess. There are various other versions.

To the right is Maria's Christian altar, located in a ceremonial room in her home. Above is her Mayan altar outside her home. Maria commonly conducts ceremonies that incorporate both sites, sequentially.

Mayan Cofradias of Atitlan
Courtesy of Samuel R. Morgan

Scenes in the Panajachel Market
Courtesy of
Samuel R. Morgan

ECONOMY

The traditional economy of the Atitlan basin is essentially agrarian, supplemented by fishing and handicrafts. Farm goods and related products (rope, hemp and goods made from them) are produced for sustenance and market sale.

Traditionally, the most notable farm products are corn, beans, onions, avocados, and pitahaya (a cactus) fruit. Wheat, garlic, sugar cane, cucumbers, chile verde, bananas, squash, tomatoes and strawberries are also grown. Of the above, corn is by far the most important for regional consumption. Coffee, introduced to Guatemala by the Jesuits, is an important cash crop. It is given focused treatment as a subject in the following section.

The types of crops grown vary somewhat, seasonally. Corn is planted in May, at the outset of the rainy season, and harvested eight months later, in December. Many farmers live in villages and travel to nearby plots to work. Many farm parcels are small and produce little more than enough to sustain family life. Still, enough food is grown in the more productive plots to provide an abundance of fruits and vegetables for sale in markets. Between seasons many farm workers migrate to coastal plantations (*fincas*) to obtain work.

Fishing is done from a variety of types of sea-craft that include native canoes (*cayucos*) and open motor boats (commonly called *tiburoneras*). A varieties of small fish and crabs primarily serve as food for the native population. The larger Black Bass is normally sold for restaurant use.

Employment is usefully viewed in two categories, the "official" or visible sector and the "gray" sector which is unreported and untaxed. Some people work in both. In the former category, carpentry and other construction trades have become increasingly important. Increasing numbers are working in private residences for the growing population of expatriates as well as serving the traditional representation of wealthy Ladinos. There is also a sizable artisan sector which focuses on the production of textiles, decorative wood and stone carvings and, to a lesser degree, paintings. Men dominate all of the artisan fields except for textiles which is almost exclusively female. The "gray" sector includes much of the artisanry accomplished at home and a broad range of activities in the areas of sales and services, both full and part-time. For men, this includes work as gardeners, handymen, watchmen, salesmen, and restaurant help in small businesses. For women this includes work as housekeepers, laundresses, weavers, and salespeople.

Boat transportation has always, and continues to be, the principal means of travel between the communities of the Atitlan Basin. Regularly scheduled colectivos and private launches of different sizes provide a range of choices for travelers.

Tourism increasingly dominates the local economy, at least in terms of cash significance. Lake Atitlan is well-suited for swimming, fishing, recreational boating, and SCUBA diving. The steep cliffs are used for para-sailing. The volcanoes offer challenging climbs. The air is clean and the temperatures are comfortable for virtually any kind of exercise. Although the local roads are increasingly used by a growing inventory of motor vehicles, the spectacular views and challenging grades are impressive stimuli to runners, hikers, and bikers. Most tourists, however, come to shop, relax, and enjoy the scenery and the growing range of sophisticated services being offered. Consequently, a growing number of residents are working in the tourist sector for tourist agencies and in hotels and restaurants.

Fishing has traditionally been one of the occupational mainstays of Mayan men at Lake Atitlan. Today they fish essentially the same as in the past, from primitive cayucos (locally-made canoes).

This is the "people's" market of Solola. While this type of marketplace is oriented toward the needs of local communities rather than tourists, it provides an insightful glimpse of contemporary Mayan culture and is well worth a visit.

A member of *Asociacion Q'omaneel* explains how medicinal plants are grown and processed by midwives and healthcare educators at the association's site in San Juan La Laguna. Products are packaged, used for patients, and sold commercially.

Larger communities have market places. Market days vary from community to community to minimize competition and to permit the collective movement of goods between communities. Populations of smaller communities travel to towns with markets to sell and buy goods. Commercial over-water transportation is important to the lakeside economy and is conducted by large-capacity scheduled ferries and a variety of smaller private water taxis.

A customer examines a weaving being offered for sale at an artisanry exhibition at *Centro Cultural Los Encuentros* in Panajachel.

COFFEE

*G*uatemalan coffees are delightfully aromatic…The *variety and complexities of aromas reflect the ways the different soils and climate patterns combine with the high mountain altitudes to create distinct regional differences in the cup. Traditional Atitlan is the most intense of the regional coffees. It is delightfully aromatic, with a crisp, pronounced acidity, and a full body.*

- The Guatemalan National coffee Association (ANACAFE)

Agriculture dominates Guatemala's economy and coffee is Guatemala's number one agricultural export product. Much of the very best coffee comes from the Lake Atitlan Basin. The coffee grown here is largely of the type classified as *Arabica* "extra hardbean", a variant first cultivated in Ethiopa, grown here at altitudes of 5,000 – 7, 000 feet, mostly under the shade of tall Gravilea trees. Coffee is grown extensively on the Lake's north side in the Panajachel area and over a larger area on the south side between San Lucas Toliman and San Marcos La Laguna. Most of this coffee leaves the area in the hands of wholesalers, to be processed, packaged, and marketed to regional and international markets. Some stays in local community

markets to be purchased and oven-roasted or pan-fried at home. More important to visitors to Atitlan, some of the best of the Lake basin coffee is sold locally, by the bag in specialty outlets, and served by the cup in discriminating restaurants and cafés here.

Coffee, as a consumer product, is the seed of a fruit that, when ripe, has an appearance much like a cherry. In fact, in coffee growing circles, this fruit is commonly referred to as a cherry. It evolves from small, beautiful, virgin-white flowers that sprout along the branches of the coffee plant in tightly formed clusters.

While the coffee plant thrives in Guatemala it is not native to the Americas. There are three principal varieties; Arabica, Robusta, and Liberica, each with it's own sub-species. The earliest known use of all three types has been traced to the African continent and its off-shore islands. Of the three general types, Traditional Arabica beans such as the Bourbon and Typica varieties are generally considered the tastiest.

However, their cultivation requires specific environmental conditions, and they are somewhat vulnerable to disease. Robusta is the hardiest type, and it thrives under a much broader range of climactic conditions. Robusta has caught the thrust of the blame for today's coffee world market glut as well as for much of the inferior tasting coffee in the marketplace. Liberica is the least well-known of the three and has hardly been exported for commercial production.

Coffee, as a brew, is both maligned as an unhealthy, addictive drink and embraced as a mental stimulant. A balanced view of it's worth would seem to be at the "middle ground" of moderate consumption. Coffee is also a medicinal plant. It's principal physiologically active constituent, caffeine, is a key ingredient in popular migraine drugs such as *Excedrin* and Bayer's *Aspirina Forte*. The coffee plant takes both the forms of a small evergreen tree and a large shrub. By educated estimate, it first appeared in Africa about 4,000 years ago. Its earliest recorded use was by hunters who mixed it's pulverized shells with animal fat to provide stamina on long hunts.

Coffee's first recorded use as a beverage is traced to Yemen, around 600 A.D. From there, beginning in the 16th century, it spread - through a combination of international warfare, conquest, and trade - first through the Turkish and, then, the Western World. The Dutch are credited with bringing the first coffee tree to Europe in 1616. The European climate was not hospitable for its cultivation. The Dutch began growing coffee in Ceylon, Java and other overseas possessions and trading it throughout Europe where it became popular as a drink in the second half of that same century. European merchants, missionaries and other travelers began to introduce coffee to the Caribbean Basin in 1714, Brazil some 13 years later, and soon after to Venezuela.

Large scale production on the American mainland was first undertaken in Brazil in the 1830's on farms and *fazendas* (large slave plantations) and in Venezuela. The scale of coffee production in Central America, however, remained small until the mid-19th century, when Costa Rica began to set the pattern for a large-scale, export coffee industry. By then, Guatemala had suffered a serious decline in its most important export market, natural dyes, and the success of the Costa Rican coffee industry prompted the Guatemalan government to promote the growth of a coffee industry through tax concessions, transportation development, and legislation which provided inexpensive land and labor for coffee expansion.

The completion of the Panama Canal and the Panama Railway caused a shift in International commerce throughout Central America away from the Caribbean to the Pacific coast. This facilitated the development of export agriculture in regions of Guatemala most suitable for coffee production. Coffee fincas began springing up in Coban and Antigua in 1855 and soon spread to Guatemala's Pacific coastal slopes and the Atitlan basin. Here, loose, volcanic

soil and mild year-round temperatures provided an ideal climate for the arabica bean. The economic potential of coffee was quickly exploited by rich *Ladino* and foreign owners as well as humble Mayan farmers. Today, the south side of the Lake holds several large coffee *fincas* (plantations) as well as a multitude of small private plots many organized into cooperatives, the latter of which are mostly in the hands of native *Tz'utujil* Mayans. The largest coffee groves near Panajachel are at the San Buenaventura, *Finca* La Vega, and *Parque* Sta. Victoria

Some of the early family coffee *fincas* at Atitlan are now third and fourth generation. However, not all of the large coffee farms of today started as such. This fact is perhaps most notable in production patterns in the Panajachel area. *Fincas* La Vega and

Coffee bean immersion tanks and drying patios at Finca La Vega, on the outskirts of Panajachel toward San Andres Semetebaj.

San Buenaventura both began as sugar plantations and subsequently shifted to coffee. La Vega became commercially defunct in the mid-20th century and, only in its recent revival, has it focused on producing quality coffee as an important cash crop. San Buenaventura, a heavy coffee producer since the early 20th century and until recently, has since diversified and is now more characteristically a resort center oriented toward eco-tourism. *Parque* Sta. Victoria, until recently largely devoted to the lumber industry, has just begun diversifying into cash coffee production and eco-tourism. All of these enterprises now recognize the special value of organically grown coffee and the hazards of chemical fertilizers and pesticides to the environment.

Both La Vega and Sta. Victoria are in the process of developing eco-tours that showcase the production and processing of coffee. The San Buenaventura Nature Reserve incorporated this subject from the very outset as an integral part of its presentation of the Lake Basin's ecology. The San Buenaventura reception center displays tutorial depictions of the Lake's natural history and the ecological threat to the environment caused by population growth, subsistence farming techniques, and modernizing influences (e.g., use of chemicals). The display also emphasizes the positive, symbiotic relationship between shade grown coffee farming and natural flora and fauna. The Reserve's nature trails wind their way through old coffee groves that exist in harmony with native vegetation and animal life.

If you don't make your coffee from the instant stuff sold in jars, you go through at least a couple of steps to get the brew you drink. But, even if you "grind your own", as many *aficionados* do, you benefit from a labor intensive, complex effort that goes into producing the roasted beans you buy. I came to understand this by

Antique coffee depulper on display at *Centro Cultural Los Encuentros* in Panajachel.

being tutored by two Atitlan coffee experts, Betty Hannstein Adams and Mike Roberts. Betty has her own coffee *finca*, a large plantation in the *departamento* of San Marcos, some distance from Atitlan. Mike, Panajachel's premier coffee retailer, has worked in coffee production and sales from South Africa to California. His visible business here is a small café, almost hidden from tourists, on a narrow street in the old part of town. It's quaint coziness belies a much larger operation that includes sampling, purchasing, and processing gourmet beans from around the world. As Mike and I sat in his *Crossroads Café*, surrounded by a countertop roaster and other trappings, he shared with me the steps involved in producing the bean that gets and keeps so many of us stimulated each day.

One must begin by understanding that the roasted bean we "decoct" at home is the seed of a tree, naturally protected by several layers of coating which must be removed before it is roasted. The process begins with the picking of the tree's ripe red fruit, commonly called "cherries." The fruit goes into a depulper which strips away the flesh (the first layer) to expose a pair of seeds. These are the beans (called *granos* in Spanish). The beans are then immersed in water for 1 ° to 3 days. This causes a fermentation process which permits the removal of the next protective layer, the mucilage, through the subsequent steps of washing and drying. Most commonly, the beans are dried by being spread on large cement patios in full sunlight, and raked about for some days to expose all of them equally to the sun. Atitlan coffee is harvested between December and March, at the height of Atitlan's dry season.

Ideally, throughout the washing and drying processes, the beans are inspected and bad ones are removed. These steps finished, the beans are referred to as *pergamino* (parchment). The beans are then tumbled around inside a hulling machine to remove the remaining layers, first the parchment and, finally, the fine "silver skin." This accomplished, they are referred to as *oro* (gold). Finally, the coffee is roasted, generally in a drum roaster, although some Lake residents buy beans unroasted in the open market and pan-fry them at home.

There are a lot of details related to the above process that can affect the quality of the product as well as variations on how different steps can be accomplished. Some of the variations don't necessarily affect the quality of the final product. Betty Adams sells to international gourmet coffee companies to include Starbucks. To meet the highest standards, her beans are washed two or three times after being

fermented, the final wash with very clean water. The inspection process to cull out bad coffee is continuous from the time the cherries are picked until the beans are sacked. Her coffee is dried in drums, rather than sun-dried. She prefers this technique as it allows her to most predictably control temperature and uniformity in the drying process. This method is also especially suitable because of the *finca's* large volume of production. On the other hand, Wolf Muller, of Panajachel's *Finca Vega*, is quite satisfied with the terrace drying technique as his volume of production is smaller and he has an adequate natural drying area.

This machine sorts de-hulled and polished coffee beans by size and shape. It is located at *Finca Tarrales*, a coffee plantation on the southern outer rim of the Atitlan basin. This coffee finca has diversified into a nature reserve offering a variety of scenic trails and outdoor activities to include bird watching and hikes.

The number of the above steps accomplished by the coffee grower depends on the size and sophistication of the grower's operation. In the Atitlan basin, much of the coffee is grown on small plots and sold as cherries to wholesalers. Some small growers de-pulp their own coffee and ferment the beans in 55-gallon drums. Sizeable fincas, have large depulpers, fermentation tanks and drying patios.

Mike's sources of coffee around the Lake vary from the moderately large *Finca Vega* to tiny producers on the south and west shores of Atitlan. He does his own deparching and removal of the silverskin filament from the beans he buys. He also collaborates with local producers who roast their own coffee; helping them by taste testing and evaluating their products. In addition to buying small quantities of quality coffee from other regions of Guatemala, Mike imports quality beans from Africa and makes his own blends for a hardcore of discriminating local customers and frequent repeat-visitors from around the world. His clients not only come to sip his brews, but to enjoy them with the incomparable pastries made by his wife Adele in their upstairs home bakery.

While Mike Roberts coffee shop is the most sophisticated among those at Atitlan, he is not the only one here who sells and serves good Atitlan coffee. One of the charms of the Lake is that the economy still nurtures small-scale business. This is a land of backyard coffee production and consumption, where many residents and visitors are "escapees" from contemporary mass culture. While there is no modern supermarket in Panajachel, the largest of the corner grocery stores sells locally bagged coffee alongside national brands. Small "niche" restaurants on Calle Santander serve Lake-grown coffee bought from local "mini" producers. The San Buenaventura Reserve, once a significant coffee producer in Panajachel, now produces only enough to serve in its own restaurants and in a downtown family bakery.

Meanwhile, across the Lake in San Lucas Toliman, the Catholic parish finances small coffee farmers and brokers their products in a way that allows them to earn a decent livelihood. Broad recognition of the high quality of Atitlan coffee has attracted big business and drawn wholesalers to the Lake to buy beans for large-scale gourmet coffee sellers. Thus, if you can't visit Lake Atitlan in person, you can find the Lake's packaged coffee in specialty stores in Antigua and Guatemala City, often dressed in fancy gift wrapping. Beyond, Atitlan coffee is sold in gourmet coffee outlets throughout the world.

Having said this, there is still nothing quite like sipping the brew right here, in a cozy little shop in Panajachel or at one of the many little cafés or restaurants in the small villages around the Lake. Coffee is a personal pleasure and this is where you find the best of it—in its own home.

PHYSICAL & CULTURAL CHARACTER OF COMMUNITIES

The Lake basin is spread over 17 municipal districts. These municipalities (called *municipios*) incorporate a variety of small communities, some lakeside and others close-by. Many of the lakeside communities are connected by road but the most prevalent form of contact between many of them is by watercraft.

Characteristically, communities are formed of an assortment of tightly spaced, mostly simple, single story structures that extend in random patterns along narrow streets and alleys from a central marketplace. The more important of the roadways are paved with stone or small cement block. Buildings serve a variety of commercial and family purposes. Indigenous-style homes predominate. These are mostly traditional 1-room houses, built from an assortment of materials including stone, cement block, wood, and metal laminate. Dwellings serve for sleeping, cooking, and family gatherings and are generally distributed around patios, or cleared areas, where related activities are conducted and domestic animals are kept.

The indigenous centers of most communities are located uphill, away from the water's edge. Some of the communities have attracted a sizable expatriate population and businesses which cater to this element and to tourism. With the exception of Panajachel, these "foreign" elements are principally spread along the lakefront areas of the towns.

All of the following lakeside communities hold the status of *municipio:* except three, which are under the municipal authorities indicated.

PANAJACHEL

Panajachel is located on the northeast shore of the Lake, on a broad river delta, less than 90 miles west of Guatemala City. It was settled by Mayan people before the Conquest . After the Conquest, The Franciscan Order, supported by the Spanish Crown, used Panajachel as a missionary base for the northern side of the Lake. It was originally named "San Francisco de Panajachel." Its contemporary importance as an international resort eclipses the general economic importance of the other towns around the Lake.

Panajachel is Kaqchikel for "place of the *Matasanos.*" The *Matasano* is a fruit tree native to the Lake credited with an amazing array of curative powers. As well as being used for treating diarrhea, fever and burns, it has been prescribed for such diverse

View of Panajachel from the highground along a hiking trail at Finca La Vega.

maladies as arteriosclerosis, arthritis, rheumatism and heart disease. While Panajachel is the historic seat of Catholic influence on the north shore of the Lake, it is the only sizeable town on the Lake that has not maintained a saint's name as part of its modern identity. This is but one of a panoply of internal cultural contradictions one finds here.

The town's official population is roughly eleven thousand. Its inhabitants are a mix of indigenous, Ladino, and expatriates (mostly North American and European.) These numbers are swelled by part time residents and the international tourist trade. The indigenous element constitutes about 70% of the stable population. Guide book assessments of the town are generally ambivalent. This is not surprising as "Pana" incorporates both the best and the worst of what a tourist destination can offer. Most of its qualities are positive and provide the visitor a range of ways to enjoy a vacation or otherwise explore Mayan or Latin culture. The town is rich in creature comforts, shopping opportunities, and places to relax. There are banks, internet cafes, restaurants, hotels, and night

spots, with a variety that serves every taste. It's cheaper to eat, drink, and stay here than in the Capital or Antigua - and the air is cleaner. Still, Panajachel's special value is not as a destination, but as a gateway to Lake Atitlan and a springboard to a myriad of experiences the Lake offers - in the water, in the smaller lakeside communities, and along the roads and trails in-between. If you're looking for more serenity than you can find in town, you only have to travel to the town's edge, or hop a boat at the dock to somewhere else. The lake has a full range of water sports (including SCUBA). The cliffs offer para-sailing. The steep hills and volcanoes offer exercise, challenge, and fantastic views. Panajachel is also near and centrally-located to some notable eco-tourism facilities.

Although the initial impression and superficial character of the town is international, "Pana" is still in many ways a Mayan community. No one is sure when or who first inhabited the place. By the time the Spanish arrived, the original population had been absorbed by competing Kaqchikel and Tz'utujil groups. Around 1524, the Kaqchikels and Spaniards joined in a major battle, defeating the Tz'utujils. Panajachel became formally Kaqchikel, under the Spanish Crown. The post-Conquest history of the town is largely one of serving as the Spanish colonial center on the northern shore of the lake for managing the consolidation of the Mayans into discreet communities. This concentration process was to "socialize" and Christianize the natives as well as to facilitate the extraction of local resources to enrich colonists and the Spanish Crown. Beyond that, the

This sketch was printed in 1892 under the title "Atitlan Desde el Norte-Noreste (Panajachel) Como Se Ve: Vulkane Central Amerikas," by Karl von Seebach, Gottingen.

Mayans were pretty much left to their meager remaining resources. Not much changed here in the way of power dynamics after Independence through most of contemporary history.

The only significant monument to the colonial period is a large Franciscan-built church that reflects the contribution of this religious order to the region's early history. It was built in 1567 and is, arguably, the most impressive Spanish colonial structure near the Lake. The church is named in honor of St. Francis of Assisi, the town's patron saint. Saint Francis is honored in a week-long festival at the beginning of October. Curiously, the town's municipal building and plaza are to the rear of the church. The asymmetry of this layout is just one example of the community's random development.

Although a slow but steady influx of affluent outsiders began to acquire property and build here beginning in the 1930's, Panajachel remained little known to the modern Western World until restless wanderers began to popularize the place in the late 1960's. Some of them found they could make a living in exporting native artisanry. The resultant demand sparked a growth spurt in the local economy. In the late 1970's, revolutionary violence scared a lot of the newcomers away. Commercial activity contracted. But, as the danger subsided, many of those who left came back, along with a new wave of outsiders. Construction and commercial activity resumed and snow-balled uncontrolled.

These conditions and events have nurtured a community that is a physical hodge podge; a kaleidoscope of thematically disparate attractions, some of which appeal to the sophisticated set and family groups and others which appeal more to tattooed, body piercing kids and swinging singles.

Members of the local culture committee discussing awards to be given at the town's annual art competition, held annually to coincide with the Feast of St. Francis of Assisi.

Panajachel has no architecturally attractive downtown area. The town's center is hard to define as it differs somewhat between the perspectives of resident and tourist activities. The Catholic church generally marks the town center for residents. The outdoor food market and city hall are close by. The town's market is open daily, with principal market days on Thursday and Sunday. The course of Santander street is the center of tourist activity. This is where one finds the largest concentration of shopping stalls, stores, and tourist-oriented restaurants. The relatively new *Museo Lacustre Atitlan*, located at the foot of Calle Santander (on the property of the Hotel Posada de Don Rodrigo), houses a professionally organized collection of rare underwater archeological artifacts recovered from the Lake's depths. One street parallel to Santander is Calle Rancho Grande. The town's most sophisticated commercial art gallery, the *Galeria,* is located here.

The outskirts of Panajachel also contain some eco and cultural attractions of note. The closest to downtown is *Los Encuentros Posada y Centro Cultural*. *Los Encuentros* is a tour and study center that boasts the best tutorial medicinal herb garden in the Lake basin. The Center also offers quality lodging and arranges hiking and cultural tours around the Lake, most ranging from 1/2 day to overnight in duration but some longer. *Los Encuentros* is a 10-minute walk from downtown, just off the exit road to Sta. Catarina.

Two others places, *Finca La Vega* and *Parque Ecologico Santa Victoria*, offer hiking and horseback riding on trails that pass through planted groves and natural woods. Both places are along the exit road toward San Andres Semetebaj, 20 and 25 minutes walking distance, respectively, from town center. *La Vega offers* horseback instruction, English-style. However, one can rent horses there equipped to ride either English or Western styles. At *Sta. Victoria* the riding style is Western. *La Vega* offers coffee tours of their *cafetal* and of their depulping, washing, and drying facilities. *La Vega* also has a tennis court and fishing ponds.

The San Buenaventura resort complex is the largest tourist attraction in the Panajachel vicinity. It lies in a valley near the bottom of the spiraling descent from Solola. Over the course of its contemporary human history, the valley has evolved from a coffee plantation into a resort complex of hotels and restaurants, anchored by the attraction of a wooded lakeshore site and a nature reserve developed by the valley's owners.

The Nature Reserve's stated goals are to educate and carry out environmentally sound and sustainable alternatives to traditional land use in Guatemala. The owners of the Hotels Atitlan and San Buenaventura have been pioneers in the application of sound waste

Above, local school students participating in an art work shop at *Los Encuentros Posada y Centro Cultural.* Below, the addition of a Mayan mural to the Center's walls.

management through initiatives such as the installation of bio-digester systems to handle sewage produced by their facilities. The Butterfly Sanctuary of the complex is probably the best known of San Buenaventura's features.

Pasture and corral areas at *Parque Ecologico Santa Victoria.* The park offers both unguided and guided trail rides as well guided hikes on an impressive network of trails.

The medicinal herb garden at *Los Encuentros Posada y Centro Cultural.* This garden contains over 30 medicinal plant varieties found around the Lake. Each plant is located in a discreet bed and identified by a sign. All are cross-referenced in a locally produced reference book that provides technical and practical information for growing, processing and using each plant.

A hiking group on a mountain trail at *Finca La Vega.* Some of this *finca's* trails have been improved to provide horse access to high elevations with great views of Panajachel and Lake Atitlan.

This is a large, screened walkthrough area holding more than 35 species of butterflies native to Guatemala. Its gardens contain a plethora of blossoming flowers and a ramada with living displays of the butterfly life-cycle. The Reserve's well-kept trails are bordered by a broad range of native flora indigenous to the Lake region The trees are labeled with their Latin and native names.

Above is the entrance to the San Buenaventura Natural Reserve. To the right is a sauna at the adjacent Hotel San Buenaventura, imaginatively built using local field stone, and used glass bottles.

Spider monkeys make their home in a section of tall trees visible from an observation deck.

There is an herb garden with a broad range of native plants.

The Hotel San Buenaventura, adjacent to the Reserve, provides an ideal complement to a visit to the Reserve. It has a restaurant and a classy swimming pool with patios that look out onto a priceless view of the Lake. This hotel has preserved the coffee land it was built on so that guests can stroll among fruit-bearing Arabica coffee trees and the stately Gravilea shade trees which provide the essential shade for the gourmet-quality coffee grown here. The nearby Hotel Atitlan also has wonderful views and holds a large botanical garden with over 2,000 species of plants.

Above are the Hotel San Buenaventura's swimming pool, shoreline and beach, developed with attention to maintaining the location's natural ambience.

SANTA CATARINA PALOPO

Santa Catarina is a small hillside community a few miles from Panajachel and connected to it by a paved road. *Palo* is Spanish for "arbol". *Po* comes from the Kaqchikel word for "amate", a type of native tree. Sta. Catarina's area is confined by the steep cliffs that surround it. Villas and stylish homes line the road and the hills around the town and lakeside. Santa Catarina has a small picturesque white church just above its small plaza. The church's age is uncertain but, Its bell is date-stamped 1762. A variety of shops, galleries, and small stores are also clustered around the plaza and along the road leading into town. There is a large resort hotel in town and a couple of smaller upscale hotels on its outskirts, along the road to San Antonio Palopo.

The town's population is about 2,900 and is almost entirely indigenous. The colorful dress of the people and the quality of their artisanry make this community especially interesting. Costumes are distinguished by rich blues (turquoise), greens, and purples in zigzag design.

The town's patroness is *La Virgen Sta. Catarina de Alejandria.* Its annual fiesta is celebrated November 24 to 26.

Inside a gallery just off the town square of Sta. Catarina.

SAN ANTONIO PALOPO

The world is full of places named San Antonio. So, the attachment of the hybrid word *Palopo* to this traditional and overwhelmingly indigenous lakeside town provides it distinction. This San Antonio is a terraced town with winding roads and walkways rising steeply up from a beautiful shoreline.

San Antonio is 7.5 miles from Panajachel and connected to it by the road through Santa Catarina. It is a picturesque, paved road that winds, climbs and plunges heading southeast along the lakeshore. San Antonio lies in a natural amphitheater shaped by surrounding slopes. Physically, it is about four times larger than Santa Catarina The town's population is roughly 10,500, about 92% indigenous. The dress of the native women is distinguished by a colorfully multicolored silk *banda* in the hair. The men here wear red woven shirts and short woolen skirts. The men's shirts are of the same color and striping as the women's blouse. San Antonio is less touched by the influence of modern society than Panajachel and Santa Catarina. It is a "day" trip for most visitors, as there is little in the way of lodging that suits the tastes of foreign

travelers except for *Las Terrazas Del Lago*. The *Terrazas* is a comfortable, relatively modern hotel. It is a good springboard for boat trips on market days to San Lucas Toliman (Sundays, Wednesdays and Fridays). San Lucas is a large market town not accessible by scheduled boat service from Panajachel.

Since the time of the Spaniards arrival, San Antonio has been populated by the Kaqchikel Mayans although its site was initially a Tz'utujil outpost and was also occupied by the Quiche for periods before the Spanish.

Archeologists have uncovered evidence of an important early ceremonial center near the extant town

To the right is a view of San Antonio from the rim road above it.

government seat, but nothing has been marked or put on display for the layman or curious traveler. Prior to the Spanish Conquest, most of the lakeside population was relatively decentralized. Mayan commoners lived in *aldeas* (hamlets), mostly in extended kinship groups. Spanish civil and religious authorities consolidated the Kaqchikels and Tz'utujils for purposes of control and assimilation. The Catholic Church (especially the Franciscans) played the critical role in the process around Atitlan. The two major Franciscan centers were Panajachel and Solola. San Antonio fell under the jurisdiction of the *Convento de Panajachel*. The town has a picturesque colonial period church. It quickly catches the eye as one rounds the road curve that begins the steep descent into the *pueblo*. The old carved statuary inside the church is interesting and well-maintained. As is the case throughout the Mayan world, the *Antoneros* (as the Locals are called) never completely abandoned their native religion. Traditional worship is still practiced in a cave site known as *El Barranco Blanco*. Don't look for signs to its location. It's not intended to be a tourist attraction.

There are few signs of foreign influence in San Antonio. A notable exception is that of Ken Edwards, a Missouran who humbly calls himself a potter. Actually, Ken is much more. He is an innovative, university-trained ceramic engineer/artist who brought Mexican kiln-fired stoneware techniques to this remote Mayan town and generated a cottage industry here of major importance.

Beyond Ken, the cottage pottery industry, and the old Catholic Church, there is more to enjoy here if you are interested in weaving and like to hike. Along the town's convoluted roads and pathways, you will bump into mostly shy but friendly people and a traditional home weaving industry in action, with traditional manually-operated looms, often in view in the front yards of homes.

In addition to growing the typical vegetable products, the community specializes in the growth of anise, the weaving of indigenous textiles, the production of maguey and its fiber, and in the fabrication of reed mats. The town's market days are Wednesday and Saturday. The town's patron is Saint Anthony of Padua. Its annual fiesta, in his honor, is June 13-14.

SAN LUCAS TOLIMAN

San Lucas is one of the larger towns on the Lake and more bustling than most. It is a commercial center for coffee growing and processing. It is located alongside Volcano Toliman and is a departure point for climbs of this volcano and Volcano Atitlan. The town is connected to the Pacific branch of the Pan American highway by paved road and to Panajachel by road and ferry. It's population is approximately 21,500, with about 88% indigenous.

The word "Toliman" is indicative of the influence of native Mexicans who accompanied Pedro Alvarado in the Spanish conquest of Guatemala. One explanation of the word's meaning is that it was named in honor of an early Toltec Chief, *Tol man*. Before the arrival of the Spanish and their allies, San Lucas was Tz'utujil territory. The population in the area was consolidated by the Spanish around 1540 and assimilation of the natives was largely accomplished by Franciscans based in Santiago. The town experienced a significant population growth spurt at the end of the nineteenth century with the introduction of the coffee industry here. Today, the population is predominantly Kaqchikel but local speech still reflects the early Tz'utujil influence.

The town has one of the larger and more architecturally elaborate Spanish colonial period churches around the Lake. Oddly, it is not on the town plaza, but rather closer to the lakeshore along the main road leading there. I was told by the Church's rector that the original plaza was closer to the church but was destroyed by fire. The church has a large dome and a spacious interior with a rich collection of statuary. No one, locally, seems to know who constructed the church or when. It bears design similarities to a seventeenth century Franciscan-built church at Concepcion, Solola and probably dates to the sixteenth or seventeenth century. It is logically Franciscan.

The parish is sponsored by a Catholic Diocese in Minnesota and has a tradition of being staffed by U.S.-born priests who stay for some time. As of this writing, the incumbent rector is Rev. Greg Schaeffer. He arrived here in 1963. Largely because of this tradition of stability and the pro-active disposition of the rector, the church has played a major role in improving the local quality of life in terms of housing, education, and medical care. The Catholic parish of St. Lucas has come to be the best destination for foreign visitors with tangible skills interested in donating personal energy to improving a poor community.

San Lucas is at the base of the twin Volcanoes *Toliman* and *Atitlan*. If you're considering climbing one of these two giants, this town is the most natural departure point. However, as of this writing, there is little local advertising for volcano climbs or any other kind of tourism. With patient inquiry, volcano guides can be found. These are mostly overnight ventures and require a lot of stamina. But, in clear weather, the views can be worth the effort. As with virtually all of the volcano climbs in Guatemala, there is some risk of assault and robbery.

San Lucas dominates a small picturesque bay. The shorefront has great views, and it is easy to visualize its potential as a natural tourist destination. But the town is lean on tourist- attractive restaurants, hotels. and the artisanry that is abundant in places like Panajachel and Santiago Atitlan. If you decide to "overnight" in San Lucas and want to stay first-class, there is a marina-resort on the same street as the church, nearer the water. The resort has a nice swimming pool and stunning landscape. Rooms and suites are luxurious. In front of it, closer to the lakeshore, is an economy alternative - a very large and rustic structure built out of locally quarried stone. While still under construction (or perhaps expansion), it has plenty of rooms. Both of these hotels have full-service restaurants and friendly management. Otherwise, don't expect much else in the way of facilities focused on tourism.

The town's market is open daily, with principal market days on Tuesdays and Fridays.

You can get to San Lucas by boat or access San Lucas by road, either via the Godinez intersection near Lake Atitlan or by the Pacific coastal highway, via the Cocales intersection. You can also get there by road from Santiago Atitlan. If you are an adventurous hiker, there are also trails connecting San Lucas with San Antonio and Santiago. If you are inclined to travel the Lake by boat stops (the best way, if you have the time to see it all), you might want to think of San Lucas as a link between San Antonio Palopo and Santiago Atitlan.

CERRO DE ORO

This small settlement, with an official population of less than a thousand people, is under the authority of Santiago Atitlan, although physically separated from it by two miles. It is located at the base of a prominent hill of the same name. Its name translates from Spanish as "hill of gold." Local legend holds that there is treasure buried in the hill. It is a geographically unique feature, nestled like a dwarf volcano at the feet of Toliman and Atitlan, along the lakeshore. It offers great views of the lake and countryside and is an easier hiking challenge than it's bigger brothers.

Popular history says the village's inhabitants are descendents of migrants from Patzicia who speak Kaqchikel. However, today, most of the fulltime residents speak Tz'utujil. The community also boasts a large population of weekend and holiday residents – mostly wealthy Guatemalans from the capitol who have built luxurious vacation homes on the village's edge.

The community has a large new church which is unremarkable except for a modern mural depicting Christ in the purple and white-striped trousers of Santiago Atitlan. There are many signs of rapid change in Cerro de Oro. There is a great deal of new building construction. There is a small but well-developed modern beach facility, with pit toilets, and shaded picnic tables and chairs. The beach has a car parking lot and a caretaker at the facility daily.

The community's traditional principle economic activities are fishing, farming, and the fabrication of reed mats (petates). However, today, many local people are employed in construction activities and as workers in the homes of the wealthy on the community's outskirts.

SANTIAGO ATITLAN

Santiago is the largest of the lakeside communities and is the principal population center of the Tz'utujils. Its population is over 32,000, with about 95% indigenous. The town is located on an embankment of broken lava at the foot of Volcano Toliman, across the bay from the pre-Conquest Tz'utujil capital.

Santiago is traditionally a fishing and farming community, known for the manufacture of *cayucos*. Coffee and garden vegetables (especially tomatoes) are the most important crops. It also has a significant artisan population. Artisans specialize in oil and tempera paintings, woodwork, and weavings. Their wares are sold from the considerable number of local shops and by wandering salespeople. Much of the weaving incorporates the distinct colors and designs of the town. Men's pants and women's huipiles in Santiago are made of embroidered, white and purple-striped material. Many women also wear a head band (*tocoyal*) of red cloth.

Santiago was founded at its current site in 1547 by Franciscans as part of the strategy to consolidate populations at convenient locations for indoctrination and management. Santiago was made one of the two principal secular, municipal-level government structures (called *corregimientos*) in the early post-conquest period. The town has a Franciscan-built (1568) Catholic church which overlooks the main plaza. The church is named in honor of Saint James the Apostle, the town's patron saint. The interior decoration incorporates Mayan as well as Catholic symbolism. The wooden pulpit is decorated by carvings of Yum-Kax, the Mayan god of corn, and that of a Quetzal bird reading a book. The town's annual fiesta is July 25, in honor of Saint James.

The religious character of the town is flavored by the veneration of Maximon, a syncretic quasi-deity that combines the identities of a pre-Columbian god, Mam, the Christian Saint Simon, the conquistador Pedro Alvarado, and the villain Judas Escariot. The town's statue of Maximon is continually feted with gifts of liquor and cigars which are considered important accessories to his dress. The figure is passed among the homes of the members of the *cofradia* that venerates him and is maintained on public display. Tourists can visit Maximon for a small entry fee, For a small additional donation, you can take his photo. It is even possible to obtain the services of a local shaman to have *Maximon* intercede in your behalf through a ceremony in the statue's presence. See Appendix 5 for more on the religious and cultural significance of this unique character. Maximon is incorporated into a variety of broader religious ceremonies.

Above left is view of San Lucas Toliman as viewed from the high ground to the east. On the flat sloping ground behind San Lucas (on the right) is the prominent hill mass of Cerro de Oro.

To the left is a typical house on a village street in Cerro de Oro.

Scenes at Santiago Atitlan.

At left is a lineup of *cayucos.*

At right is a traditionally attired Mayan woman with her granddaughter. The young girl has traded her *huipil* for a Western-style T-shirt.

He is especially honored on Wednesday through Friday of Holy Week.

Tourist literature places a facility named the *Parque Nacional Atitlan* a little more than a mile north from Santiago. It is described as a bird reserve for the Atitlan Poc (grebe). This place is not, as its name implies, a significant tourist attraction. The most interesting physical attraction in the area of cultural tourism is the *Weaving Center and Museum Cojol* ya *Association.* This center presents the evolution of textiles of Santiago Atitlan as well as the backstrap weaving technique generally practiced by traditional Mayan weavers. The Center is located in a small building just 50 meters from the Santiago dock. Its limited interior is completely and efficiently utilized with informative displays accompanied by written explanations in English and Spanish. Also housed inside is a small shop where the Association sells products made by members.

Tourists interested in being guided to explore the natural and archeolgical dimensions of the Santiago area can contact *"Aventuras en Atitlan"*, a small but professional horseback riding and hiking company run by an Arizona, USA expatriate couple. They operate their business from their residence along the road running southwest from Santiago. Room and board is also offered on site. Those interested in learning more specifically about traditional Tz'utijil culture can contact Delores Ratzan, a local Tz'utujil woman who has traveled internationally while maintaining deep roots in local culture.

There is an upscale hotel on the southern edge of town, the Posada Santiago. If you are already in Santiago and interested in contacting either Delores Ratzan or *Aventuras en Atitlan*, the management of the Posada Santiago can help you. There are a few basic tourist-oriented hotels in town and a couple of other hotels on the northern edge. Probably the best of the latter is the Bambu. The Posada Santiago and the Bambu have their own docks and can also be reached by a water "taxi" from the Santiago dock.

Santiago's market days are Friday and Sunday.

SAN PEDRO LA LAGUNA

San Pedro is a mid-sized, densely populated community situated in the skirts of San Pedro Volcano. Its population of nearly 10,000 is 98% Tz'utujil. It was founded as a Spanish colonial settlement somewhere between 1547-50 and as a *pueblo* around 1575-85. Its original name was San Pedro Patzununa. Other than a noisy and colorful celebration in honor of its patron saint June 29 - 30 every year, San Pedro is a rather "laid-back" place,with traditional society dominating the high ground and tourism reigning on the lakeshore. The local citizens are called *Pedranos*.

The town's pre-Columbian history is steeped in Tz'utujil legend. This rich informational source competes with the most imaginative works of the literary genre called Magical Realism Legend says that, during the Spanish Conquest, a group of some 20 virgin maidens of the Tz'utujil kingdom of Tzanchanay were fleeing capture by the Spanish *Conquistadores*. At the point that things appeared hopeless, they hurled themselves from a precipice of the San Pedro Volcano, preferring suicide to dishonor. In their fall, the local spirits intervened and the maidens were transformed into white pigeons. Soaring exuberantly upward from their encounter with death, these transformed winged creatures skirted the shoreline around the volcano to discover the site which would become the future San Pedro.

Aside from its cultural significance, *Volcan San Pedro* is economically important to the *Pedranos* . Coffee and corn are grown well up its slopes. Its trees furnish construction material and firewood for stoves.

Volcan San Pedro is also the easiest of the three lakeside volcanoes to climb and, if you're in good shape, you can "top" it in about four hours. Besides the exercise value, and assuming clear weather, you'll experience spectacular views. Of course there is some risk. If you decide to climb it, invest in a good local guide.

This town has something for everyone. And, while it lacks star-rated hotels, it's an easy day trip from the luxury of Panajachel. For the budget-minded, young-at-heart traveler San Pedro is an especially appealing place to stay. It's full of cheap but good hotels and restaurants. As of this writing, you can still get *a Cuba Libre* for six Quetzales at a lakefront restaurant with great views and an international menu. The town has Spanish schools, horseback riding, a good nearby beach, outdoor collective hot tubs, and funky hang-outs. It also has Mayan culture, accessible *curanderos*, and indigenous artists who have gained international fame.

The spirits of the Lake and the Volcano are central to a host of captivating stories that relate the intervention of supernatural will in the historic evolution of native history. The complex indigenous belief system also imaginatively blends early Mayan with post Conquest Christian teachings in a way that gives strong credence to the powers of Shamanism. The most colorful of *Pedrano curanderos* is a locally well-known and respected elder named Feliciano Pop Gonzalez. Feliciano is an ardent Roman Catholic who administers what he describes as a God-given gift for curing, mostly from the private chapel of his home. He also operates a "museum for the poor" where he sells hand-carved stone artifacts to help fund education for local youth. If you speak some Spanish or are traveling with someone who does, Feliciano is well-worth a visit. He likes foreigners.

"Gonzalez" is part of the name of most prominent artists of the *Arte Naif* or *Primitiva* school in San Pedro (I counted 11 Gonzalez painters of some prominence from the town.) On one of my first visits, without appointments, I met two of these men in their own business establishments which, in each case, housed a personal work studio, a display gallery, and a restaurant. One of them, Emilio Gonzalez Morales, takes special pride in the uniqueness of his paintings done from a perspective vertically above his subjects. Some of his pieces were quite attractive. But, I was especially impressed by a work in progress showed to me by his fellow *Pedrano,* Pedro Rafael Gonzalez. It was a nativity scene that syncretically portrayed a Mayan God child in generally the same manger setting as that used for the Christ child, but with distinctive symbolism. Pedro Rafael's work is recognized internationally and has been exhibited in the United

States. Other *Pedrano* painters, and most notably Mariano Gonzalez Chavajay, can also claim this distinction.

Even beyond *curanderos* and artists, the appellation "Gonzalez" has found its way into most every *Pedrano's* name. According to a local monograph I was shown, this peculiarity stems from the sudden arrival, many generations ago, of an "audacious" Spanish adventurer named Antonio Mariano Gonzalez. This first Gonzalez was said to be "on the run" from Totonicapan with a young Quiche woman. The pair were lovers, fleeing the woman's home town under speculative circumstances. The two took refuge in San Pedro and, over the years, this first Gonzalez became a respected community leader. Somehow, he passed on his name to just about everybody in the town.

Beyond coffee and corn, fruit and avocado production are also significant. The production of shirts, rugs, and curios for the tourist market is an important economic part of the town's economic life.

The town's principal market days are Thursday and Sundays but don't plan your visit around these; the market is not tourist-oriented and you can buy the local textiles and curios produced in San Pedro when in Panajachel, for about the same price.

If you're driving, the roads accessing San Pedro have improved dramatically in recent years. But, for most, the boat ride from Panajachel still makes more sense.

SAN JUAN LA LAGUNA

San Juan is San Pedro La Laguna's "little brother". It is located, lakeside, immediately to its west. Its 8,000 plus inhabitants are almost exclusively Tz'utujil. The community's original Spanish colonial name was San Juan Bautista. It was given the status of *pueblo* somewhere around 1618-23. It's name was modified to its present form around that time.

The town's pre-conquest history is fuzzy. Evidence of pre-Columbian Mayan presence was uncovered by Archeologist Samuel K. Lathrop in 1932. Lathrop discovered a cluster of mounds near the town's present location ranging up to 4.6 meters high, forming a ceremonial plaza. Stone sculpture, still visible in the town's plaza at that time was dated to the Late Post-classic Period (a.d. 1200 – 1524). None of this remains.

After (and despite) the Spanish Conquest, conflict between Mayan peoples over territory persisted. This competition prompted the Tz'utujils to reinforce their population at San Juan to counter Quiche expansion from the north.

Except for the nearby attractive Cristalinas beach, which is about half-mile away at the back of a sweeping lagoon, San Juan hardly gets mention in tour guides. However the town holds things of special interest to those interested in eco and cultural tourism. Besides Las Cristalinas (one of the best sandy beaches on Atitlan's shoreline), San Juan boasts resident master artists who work in oil on canvass in the genre of *Arte Naif* and weavers, some of the latter who tint their works exclusively in natural dyes derived from plants found in the Atitlan basin.

Because of the lack of a tourism infrastructure, these attractions are difficult to locate without a guide or the discretionary time and Spanish language capacity that allows one to independently search out these artists' and artisans' workshops and outlets. This is changing, with specific projects in-progress supported by outside help, designed to develop tourism infra-structure.

Traditionally, for tourists, San Juan has been a logical side trip when visiting San Pedro. It is a 25-minute strenuous hike from the center of one town to the other. The little-trafficked, paved road between the two communities is flanked by young coffee trees and offers great views of the Lake. If you want to travel this road without walking, small pick-up trucks provide collective taxi service to San Juan (and beyond). At the entrance to San Juan, and below the road toward the shore, is the eco-lodge Uxlabil Atitlan. It is the only upscale tourist lodging in San Juan. It has its own dock, between San Pedro's and San Juan's public docks.

San Juan's public dock is only a few minutes from San Pedro's Panajachel dock. (Remember, San Pedro has separate docks for accessing Panajachel and Santiago Atitlan.) There is a great view of the Lake, from the foot of the San Juan dock, looking out along the dock's rustic and rickety length. The road uphill from the dock to the town center is flanked by a lush mix of corn, coffee and banana trees. It leads to a little square dominated by the Catholic Church. The church shelters some impressive old statuary.

On the right side of the road, leading up from the dock, is *Hospedaje Estrella de Lago*. It's a modern but basic hotel, with shared baths only. A second story is in the process of being built. It may, eventually, offer

Cultural Activities San Juan La Laguna

Above left, Rosa Mendoza of weavers COOP LEMA demonstrates how thread is organized to prepare it for weaving on a backstrap loom.

Above right, she shows process of dying the thread using local natural plant materials.

At left is a display of natural plant products made and sold locally by the *Asociacion de* Comadronas y Educadoras de *Salud de San Juan Q'omaneel* (Association of midwives & Healthcare Educators).

At right, artist Felipe Ujpan demonstrates his style and technique to a visitor in his home studio and gallery.

private baths. This *hospedaje*, the local chain eatery *Nick's Place* (pizza and sandwich fare), a post office, and a bank (*Banrural*), that exchanges dollars and cashes travelers' checks, are the only tourist conveniences in town beside eco-lodge Uxlabil, as of this writing.

San Juan has remained a small farming and fishing town through its recorded history. Artisans have traditionally specialized in the weaving of reed mats (*petates*) and textiles. However, as mentioned above, the textile weaving being done by women's cooperatives here is quite sophisticated. The quality of the handiwork is especially significant considering the weavers continue to use looms and associated human-powered devices of designs that date back centuries.

The workshop area of *Asociacion Artesanos* contains an impressive assortment of locally made foot looms, still in use. The cooperative includes some 200 women. The women are grouped into a variety of specialties to make products ranging from carry bags and rugs to jackets and bed covers. Most of the work is sold to wholesalers for export to the United States and Europe. However, the *Asociacion* also sells retail to passing visitors. There are other, smaller women's groups here that sell their products from their own outlets in the streets of Panajachel and in *Centro Nim P'ot* in Antigua. Most impressive of these from a cultural standpoint is *La Associacion de Mujeres Tejedoras Con Tinte Natural (LEMA)*, a group which make the dyes they use for weaving from Atitlan Basin plants.

The evolution of a group of indigenous artists who paint in oils is a relatively recent phenomenon, sparked by the influence of the "Primitivist" oil painters of San Pedro. Among the best known of the San Juan artists are Felipe Ujpan Mendoza and Antonio Coche Mendoza who, along with Antonio Vasquez Yojcom and Diego Isaias Hernandez, two other accomplished painters, have formed an association structured around galleries located in their own residences. Another well known artist is Antonio Ixtamer, a student of San Pedro master painter Pedro Rafael Gonzalez. Antonio's paintings and those of Felipe Upjohn, Antonio Coche, and Victor Vasquez Temo are featured in the UNESCO/BANCAFE -published *Arte Naif; Guatemala*. This book has since been re-published twice. The 3d printing is a bilingual (English-Spanish) edition.

All of the aforementioned artists as well as their fellow *San Juanero* artist Chema Gonzalez Cox have had their work exhibited in the United States. The accomplishments of some of these artists are discussed in further detail in Appendix 2.

Felipe Ujpan's and Antonio Coche's galleries are near town center. Antonio Vasquez's home is just off to the left of the road heading into San Juan's center from the dock. It's just beyond the sign pointing down a rutted dirt trail to the *Asociacion Artesanos de San Juan.*

Diego Isaias' gallery is on the edge of town in the direction of San Pedro La Laguna.

Market day is Thursday. The town's principal feast day is June 22.

SAN PABLO LA LAGUNA

San Pablo is a Mayan Tz'utujil community of almost 6,000 people on the west side of the Lake, between San Juan and San Marcos. It is about seven miles by water from Panajachel. San Pablo is at the site of a pre-Colombian settlement but is said to have been founded as a community by the Franciscans between 1547 and 1559.

San Pablo is not high on anyone's list of notable tourist sites. Still every village on the Lake has something unique to offer. This community specializes in the growth and processing of maguey and the fabrication of products from it, e.g., hammocks, nets, bags, ropes, and other articles. It has some interesting alternative medicine resources. Another attraction for some is the town's close proximity to *Las Cristalinas* Beach.

The first time I visited San Pablo was by car, via a newly paved road beginning along the Pan American Highway, between the highway intersection called Los Encuentros and the city of Quetzaltenango. This Lake access road is torturously convoluted and steep but with spectacular lake and volcano views. San Pablo can also be reached by vehicle from the east, passing through Santiago Atitlan and San Pedro.

In contrast to the beautiful views along the land routes to the village, the physical appearance of San Pablo itself is totally unspectacular. There are no tourist facilities. Beside the nearby beach, the most interesting thing to most outsiders is the sight of villagers twisting maguey fibers into rope along the length of the town's rustic streets, employing centuries-old methods.

The townspeople are helpful to outsiders. On my first visit, I was with a friend, looking for a child

curandero who was a bone and joint healer (called a *huesero*). We were quickly provided directions to his home. We were also given offers to be introduced to *brujos* and *hechiceros* who work the darker side of the supernatural. We stuck to our original quest and learned that the boy we sought, a 15-year old, was named Luis Pablo Tuy Tuy. Pablo was in school when we arrived, but he got permission to leave to attend to my friend. Pablo told us his curative powers came to him in a dream and enabled him to heal his grandmother's arm which was broken at the time. He was five years old when this happened. He has been healing satisfied clients ever since. Pablo is a Catholic who sees his powers as God's gift. He is a physically slight, "serious beyond his age" boy – somewhat mystical. My friend felt good about the treatment she got that day and, much later, told me it had been effective.

On another outing, I visited San Pablo by boat to meet an indigenous *naturista* named Andres Culum. Andres grows and processes medicinal herbs. He has his own garden and a *farmacia* in San Pablo. He also grows plants at several other gardens he has helped to establish for groups and individuals around the Lake. A soft spoken, confident young man, Andres is also a teacher who gives talks on the use of medicinal plants. After hearing good reports on him, I incorporated him into a workshop on alternative medicine at *Los Encuentros,* my study center in Panajachel.

For most, San Pablo (like San Juan) is considered a side-stop on the way from Panajachel to San Pedro. The boats leave for these villages from the Calle del Embarcadero dock. The ride usually costs 15 Quetzales and takes about a °-hour. When you reach the San Pablo dock, you are still a strong 20-minute uphill walk from the outskirts of town. It begins on a good field stone road that encounters an asphalt road, forming a "T", after about five minutes. Make a right at the "T" and continue uphill to the town's outskirts. Or, catch a ride from the T- intersection from one of the many small pick-up trucks that run the roads around the Lake as taxis. The cost is only one Quetzal. For another Quetzal or two you can get a ride back to *Cristalinas* beach. But be prepared to "rough it". There are no beach facilities (e.g., change rooms, bathrooms, snack stands.).

The town's principal feast day is January 25. It is easy to tie a visit to San Pablo with other lakeside communities (San Juan, San Pedro, San Marcos) if you start out by boat to any one of them and follow the connecting roads between them. It's great hiking or biking. The roads are good for vehicles but stick to daylight and be careful on the curves. Many of the local drivers are reckless. The majority are the small pick-ups that provide collective taxi service and local cargo hauling between towns.

SAN MARCOS LA LAGUNA

San Marcos is a peaceful little place about six miles across the Lake from Panajachel. It can also be reached from the Pan American Highway. Its official population of over 2,000 inhabitants is 98% indigenous. The natives are called *Marquenses*.

One account dates the community's beginning as April 1584 when a Franciscan missionary celebrated a mass dedicated to *San Marcos* in the town's general location. However, according to other sources, today's population of San Marcos came to Atitlan in 1666, from an area along the coast below San Lucas Toliman; a place called Paquip in the jurisdiction of Patulul.

By some accounts, the *Marquenses* were dislodged from their original community by a plague of vampire bats which were devastating the cattle herds. A more colorful Kaqchikel version recounts that a stranger appeared in the homeland of the coastal dwellers and asked for lodging. When he was rebuffed, he became angry and magically materialized a lion who proceeded to attack the local folk and eat them. As the carnage spread, the people fled, ultimately arriving at Lake Atitlan. Legend says they roamed for three hundred years before finding vacant land between San Pablo and Santa Cruz. This latter account is more in line with a letter from a missionary, Padre Gonzalo Mendez, to King Felipe II and reports of Padre Pedro de Arboleda that the homeland of the *Marquenses* near the coast was plagued by "tigers and lions."

Whatever the cause, it seems that the *Marquenses* first tried to settle in the vicinity of Cerro de Oro but were driven off by (depending on the story) either neighbors from Santiago or bats. From there, they moved to the northwest side of the Lake, north of the community's current site. Here, there were some other readjustments. Finally, the *Marquenses* relocated from the vicinity of Jaibalito to the community's present site in 1726. In all, these people have shifted locations at least five times. The town's original name was San Marcos Paquip. Despite all the moves, this name remained into the 18th century.

There are three general demographic elements in San Marcos, with considerable porosity in the demographic boundaries. First of all, San Marcos is still very much an indigenous community and, out of respect for a history of floods, the Mayans are concentrated on the high ground. There is also a population of expatriate and Ladino entrepreneurs and vacation homeowners, who are concentrated on the lakeshore low ground. Finally, there are the minimalists (mostly expatriate), who blend with the other elements but are mostly located on the low ground.

Fish and crab catching are important traditional economic activities for the *Marquenses*. Farming specializes in tomatoes, jocotes, and citrus fruit, most significantly oranges. Tourism employs a considerable and growing number of native and expatriate residents.

For the majority of tourists, the most interesting destinations are close to dockside. Catch a boat from Panajachel at the foot of Calle del Embarcadero. There are two public docksites at San Marcos. The principal one (the second traveling in the direction from Panajachel) is adjacent to a pair of private docks belonging to Posada Schumann and Las Piramides Meditation Center. The Schumann and Piramides docks are at the foot of a labrynth-like trail network. There is an easement to the trails and there are a lot of directional signs. Most are helpful. The Schumann is a comfortable well-established hotel at the upper end of the price range for San Marcos. This doesn't make it expensive by Panajachel standards. Most of the other hotels are budget-quality with shared bath. Those which offer meals normally have a fixed, single meal menu. Some of them are very good budget bargains. There is a variety of Bohemian cafes and restaurants with limited menus but good food.

Las Piramides conducts programs that incorporate yoga, meditation, self reflection, dream analysis, astral projection, etc., for people who stay awhile. Day-trippers can enjoy the Center's vegetarian restaurant. Another "natural healing" center is Centro Holistico San Marcos which offers treatments in Reiki, various types of massage therapies, aromatherapy, and Bach flower therapy as well as teaching workshops in Reiki and massage. At any given time, San Marcos is said to have up to four practicing massage therapists. This number includes those working at Las Piramides and the Centro Holistico. The easiest independent masseuse to locate from the trailhead is Beatrice Sergent, a French woman who speaks English and Spanish and who specializes in Reiki and Shiatsu. Beatrice also offers classes in self-treatment and the treatment of others. If you are interested in shamanism, look for Aum-Rak, a bilingual woman who is experienced in a variety of Mayan and Eastern healing practices. She offers treatment in these and private instruction in neoshamanism.

Inland from and above the network of trails that access the tourist-oriented activities of the town is a car-traffic road that provides an informal boundary between the foreign and Mayan sectors of San Marcos. Relations are good between the population components, even considering the vast economic and cultural gap.

The town's principal feast day is April 25.

TZUNUNA

This is a small village close to San Marcos that belongs to it. Its name means "hummingbird of the water." The women wear beautiful red huipiles striped with blue and yellow on the back. Oranges and lemons are important market crops here.

Tzununa is connected to San Marcos by a good dirt road and beyond to the Pan American highway by a newly paved road. Until recently, the inhabitants had the reputation for being especially shy toward strangers. But things are modernizing rapidly. Roadways in the village are being paved. There is a relatively new and remarkably well-built pier, considering the community's size. Outsiders are increasingly buying land and building homes here.

SANTA CRUZ LA LAGUNA/JAIBALITO

Santa Cruz is a *municipio* of over 4,000 inhabitants, almost all Kaqchikel. Jaibalito is a small nearby village belonging to it. The two are connected by a foot trail. Its indigenous people are also Kaqchikel. These two places are the most isolated communities on the lake from the standpoint of land access. There are no roads to either of the two.

Sta. Cruz is best known for its tourist facilities which include several hotels and a SCUBA diving center. These are on the shoreline. The town itself is located beyond, a roughly 200 meter vertical climb from the dock up a steep winding road, high on the hillside. Originally on the lakeshore, the town was relocated uphill, as were some of the others around the Lake, after a series of devastating floods in the 17th and 18th centuries.

Isolation and meager usable terrain have largely shaped this pre-Columbian town's personality. The inhabitants are hardy, hard-working but mostly poor people. Illiteracy is 70 %. Crippling and life-threatening illnesses are serious problems and the town has no doctor.

The socioeconomic situation is the same in Jaibalito. This village is also perched high above the shoreline. It has a couple of lakeside hotels but is more isolated and less developed than Sta. Cruz.

In recent years, the quality of life has been improving significantly for the natives. Town leaders are working with whoever is willing to help. The Catholic Church is doing some good. Local expatriates organized as "Amigos de la Escuela" raise money and fund educational materials, support school construction/repair, supplement the school nutritional program, and provide scholarships beyond middle school. Another group of volunteers has funded a public library for the town. Streets are being paved. The street and *callejones* are fairly clean, despite a considerable population of unconstrained chickens, dogs, and ducks. Most tourists see little if any of this.

Santa Cruz La Laguna perched on the high ground, with luxurious Western-style homes below.

What does bring outsiders to Santa Cruz and Jaibalito? The very smallness of the communities and the isolation attract many; coupled with easy boat access. Santa Cruz is just to the west of Panajachel. Jaibalito is just beyond. It's only ten minutes by boat to these places at a cost of five to ten Quetzales. As you cruise the shoreline approaching their community docks, you'll see a profusion of architecturally diverse dwellings, many of them luxurious. Many have been built by North Americans and European expatriates. Others are vacation homes of rich Guatemalans. As mentioned, some of these newcomers have applied their talents toward improving the indigenous standard of living. Others are applying their talents to serve tourists who are attracted here for the refuge or retreat qualities of the environment.

Immediately off Sta. Cruz's main dock are three hotel-restaurants that draw most of the tourists; Arca de Noe, La Casa Rosa, and Iguana Perdida. They all offer plenty of comfortable garden lounge space, decent basic dining, and saunas . Boats are available for rent. The Iguana Perdida is also home of ATI Divers, a PADI certified school. There is a luxury alternative to these three, the Villa Sumaya, about 15 minutes further down the waterfront trail. For the non-athletic, the most convenient way to get there is by boat to the hotel's own dock. Boatmen know the site best by its Mayan name, *Paxanax*.

Santa Cruz is home to a number of English-speaking healers who practice specialties ranging from massage to energy therapy. Finding these people here on a given day, however, can be challenging. Santa Cruz is friendly but socially anarchic. Other than the hotels, there is little attention to commercialism. Few residents follow much of any schedule.

As of this writing Jaibalito had two tourist-oriented hotels, Casa del Mundo and the Vulcano Lodge. Both serve all meals but with a fixed dinner menu. Both offer good food and clean and comfortable lodging. Lake views from the Casa del Mundo are especially striking.

A sizeable segment of the indigenous population makes its living providing services to the newcomers and visitors. In terms of the traditional economy, orange growing is important, as well as canoe making and fishing.

The color red predominates in indigenous costumes.

The town's annual fiesta is celebrated May 7 to 11.

OTHER SIGNIFICANT NEARBY COMMUNITIES

SOLOLA

Solola is the capitol of the *departamento* of Solola, the state-equivalent governmental structure in which the Atitlan Basin is located. Solola is located 85 miles from Guatemala City and is one of the major market centers of the Western Highlands.

Solola was founded as a *pueblo* in 1547 and originally named "Tecpan Atitlan." Since it's founding, it has been the most important political city in the Lake region. Solola is the site of a contemporary diocesan cathedral, Our Lady of the Assumption. The cathedral frames one side of the central plaza. Its architecture is impressive but its furnishings are meager. Another landmark is the picturesque, turn-of-the-century (19th-20th) Central American tower, designed and constructed to stress the theme of unity between the Central American countries. Solola holds its annual fiesta between August 11 – 17.

Traditionally, men here dress in red-striped pants with blanket aprons and waist length woolen coats or jackets with distinctive bat emblems on the back. Women wear multi-hued long skirts with red pin-striped huipiles, tailored like traditional men's shirts.

Activity in Solola surges on its fixed market days on Tuesdays and Fridays, as venders from nearby villages travel here in large numbers to sell their goods.

SAN JORGE LA LAGUNA

This picturesque village, under the administration of the *municipio* of Solola, is located at the end of a recently paved side road off the main road connecting Solola with Panajachel. It is largely populated by Kaqchikel's who fled Antigua in 1773, at the time of the catastrophic earthquake there. San Jorge is one of the smaller and poorer communities associated with the Lake. Originally located on the lakeshore, it was moved to higher ground because of recurring floods. The current location offers inspiring views of the Lake.

Recently, a satellite village was re-established on the lakeshore. This development is the outgrowth of an internal squabble among the residents over the sale of the village's lowland area to outside developers. The intent of the settlement is largely to prevent development.

The village has a small but attractive Catholic church, especially worth visiting to see the collection of statuary it holds. San Jorge shares with Santiago Atitlan the distinction of being home to a venerated image of Maximon. The community's feast date is April 24, in honor of the feast day of its patron saint. The community's celebration includes colorful indigenous dances.

The village's most notable crop is corn.

Partial view of the façade of the ruin of St. Andrew's Church, San Andres Semetabaj.

SAN ANDRES SEMETABAJ

This small agrarian town is about 5 miles inland from Panajachel on a winding, steeply ascending paved road. It is distinguished by the impressive ruins of a Spanish colonial church.

APPENDIX 1
AN EXTENDED FAMILY CASE PROFILE

Manuel Gonzalez Navichoc is a 74-year old Tz'utujil who has lived all his life in San Pedro La Laguna. He speaks only his native language. I interviewed Manuel in Spanish through a granddaughter, Rosa. Rosa is a "modern" Tz'utujil who, because of a personal hardship, was forced to spend much of her early life away from Atitlan. Although her views are not entirely typical of her people, she maintains the visible customs, at least in public. Rosa reads and writes in Spanish. Like many other young Tz'utujils, she speaks her own language and Spanish fluently. She also speaks some Kaqchikel.

Manuel was raised in an age where the only tools of education were story telling and an erasable board with chalk. He lives with his wife in a simple home, close to his extended family. He is in extraordinarily good health and mentally alert. Manuel's wife suffers from a chronic, undiagnosed sickness that causes outbreaks of skin sores on a cheek. It has been diagnosed as a virus, probably Herpes. At least some of her family believes it is the result of *Brujeria* (witchcraft), a curse placed on her by some unknown, envious person.

"Don Manuel" is treated with honor as an elder in his neighborhood, but he laments that respect for age has generally diminished among the Tz'utujils. He remembers a past when *ancianos* (old people) were commonly treated with great deference. He demonstrated for me with Rosa how, in his childhood, youths greeted elders by kneeling and kissing an outstretched hand. The kneeling has been replaced by a bowing from the waist and a taking of the hand that ends short of lip contact.

Manuel warmly recounts the courtship pattern of his childhood. A first encounter would commonly occur as a young woman was struggling to transport a clay water jar uphill from the lake's edge to her family home. If approached by a male, she would turn her

Manuel Gonzalez Navichoc surrounded by three generations of family members.

back to conversation unless the young man took her burden on himself and helped her home. The relationship would long be limited to polite conversation. After three years, the man could propose marriage by offering her a *moneda* (money coin). If she accepted it, she would take the coin to her parents. If they approved, the marriage would be consummated.

Manuel removes a large engraved silver medallion with chain from its keeping place and proudly shares it with me. He explains how it came to be his. About 200 years ago a relative unearthed it in nearby San Juan La Laguna while preparing a field for planting. When the man died, he passed in on to Manuel's father, as an heirloom. The medallion is about two inches in diameter and heavy. It is kept shined as if new. One face bears a sun with scroll ornamentation. The other bears a highly ornamental cross.

I asked Manuel about his understanding of the origin of the Tz'utujil people. Popular ideas vary on where these people came from before settling on the Lake. "We have always been here", was his response. I questioned him about the current relationship between the Tz'utujils and the Kaqchikels. He remembers when , in his youth, there was still some collective animosity between these two historic enemies. "It's gone" he said. We were here first but now they have their places and we have ours. When we meet, we get along."

While Manuel closely regards tradition, he appreciates the practical value of modern technology. His pants and shirt are of Tz'utujil style and cloth, but the jacket is closed with a zipper. He wears modern-style eyeglasses. He remembers a time when there was only one commercial mill accessible to the community and when women ground corn with a hand stone at home and processed it into *masa* (dough). He recalls the days before internal combustion engines when transportation was limited to the horse and *cayuco* (canoe) and when trade was limited between lakeside communities because of this circumstance and the lack of incentive to trade because everyone within a day's journey produced the same things.

Feliciano P'op explaining the mystical powers of an amulet he uses to help cure afflictions. Feliciano is a curandero, sculptor, and master story teller.

Manuel is a devout Catholic who gives little credence to religious beliefs not endorsed by the Church. The syncretic dimension of popular Catholicism is outside of his belief system and, as such, he is testimony to the diversity of faith that exists within the Mayan world. This does not prevent his acceptance of miraculous cures performed by *curanderos* (medicine men). Men and women who claim access to supernatural powers are common in Mayan culture. They frequently employ objects attributed with magical powers to accomplish their cures. Manuel considers such objects to be gifts to mankind from God rather than magic.

Long ago, his wife's grandmother came upon a *huesito* (small bone fragment) that she sensed had supernatural powers. She kept it. The *huesito* communicated to her through dreams. By wrapping the bone in cloth and passing it across an afflicted area, she learned she could perform bone and joint cures. She practiced first on family and neighbors. When her success became well known, she cured people who traveled to seek her help. After she died, the fragment stayed closely guarded within the family and continued to be used to cure injuries. It's utility is clearly linked to the talents of the possessor.

The *huesito* is currently in the hands of a nephew, Jose Quiacain Quiacain. Manuel judges Jose to be still relatively untrained in its use. Manuel assured me he had personally witnessed many cures with the *huesito* through previous practicioners. A cultural monograph published by the community in 1979 attested to the efficacy of an old woman, Rosario, in effecting cures with this fragment. Referred to as the "Viejita de Los Huesos", a caption next to her picture credits her with cures "inexplicable by modern science".

Rosa took me to visit Jose Quiacain. He was not home the first time and, so, we arranged a second visit in advance. Jose is a farm laborer who travels between work sites during the week but tries to be with his family in San Pedro on Sundays. He carries the *huesito* with him during the week as he is often asked to affect cures. He proudly points to momentos on a wall that he says are gifts from grateful clients. I asked him if his cures are instantaneous. He said "no" and that they took anywhere from a day to three months. Serious injuries sometimes took up to a year. In his treatment, he splints fractures and uses a salve that he massages over the afflicted site. He stressed that cures also required an investment of faith on the part of the person being treated.

While we were there, Rosa asked him to treat an old leg injury of hers that was a source of chronic pain. Jose inquired as to its nature. She explained that she had suffered a hard blow to the area years earlier. He probed at the location of the injury with his hand, exerting considerable pressure. He said he could feel that there had been a break. Jose removed what was supposedly the *huesito* from a shirt pocket and applied it to the area, palming it in such a way that it was completely obscured. He massaged it forcefully against her skin, back and forth for several minutes, causing her to occasionally cry out from pain. Finished, he rubbed salve into the area. Rosa paid him the equivalent of $.80 and we left. A short while later I asked her about the experience. She said the salve had produced a lingering burning sensation and that the leg still hurt but felt better than before. A week later I questioned her again about her leg . She told me the treatment had helped and she intended to visit Jose again.

The 1979 San Pedro monograph relies on legends to explain local history. The author explains that there is an absence of "… documents rescued from the hands of time," hands " … which erase all." The monograph provides the already related story about the abundant use of the Spanish name "Gonzalez" amid Tz'utujil names in San Pedro. I had become aware of the monograph from Don Manuel Gonzalez. He guards a copy closely as a cultural treasure. Interestingly, when I had earlier asked him to explain the presence of "Gonzalez" in his name, he could only tell me that it had appeared in his family about 200 years earlier . He was apparently unaware of the account in the monograph because it is written in Spanish, and no one had translated it for him. The monograph also provided me the legend of the origin of San Pedro that stems from the attempted mass suicide of the virgin maidens.

Manuel's grandaughter, Rosa, told me a folktale of about the spirits of the volcano and how, some hundreds of years ago, they punished the *Pedranos* for disrespect. I had heard this legend earlier, with slightly different details, from Feliciano P'op Gonzalez.

In this story, three mysterious young women appear in San Pedro at 2 a.m. in front of the local church. They catch the attention of local police because they are strangers and because they are being somewhat noisy late at night. Physically, the three women are strikingly different. One is dark complexioned and with black hair. Another is a blond with light skin. The third has white hair and white skin, perhaps albino. Though the three are not disturbing anyone or otherwise breaking the law, they are jailed on the charge of curfew violation.

The next morning, the deputies report the incident to their police chief who orders the women be brought before him. But, when the cell is opened, they are not there. In their place are three ears of corn, one each of brown, yellow, and white kernels. All three types of corn grow in the San Pedro region. No one knows what to make of the young women or their disappearance, beyond the growing conviction that they are manifestations of local spirits.

Shortly afterwards, a prolonged torrential rain begins which destroys all of the corn being grown in the region. The people are reduced to eating food from meal produced from the tuber of the *Chichicaste* plant. They are thus reminded of the power of the spirits of the volcano and of the importance of showing the spirits respect. Feliciano carves primitive figures out of stone from *Volcan San Pedro*. Among his works is a representation of the three legendary women. Rosa's husband, Otto, shared a folktale he learned in childhood from his father. The story's setting is the *Cerro de Oro* (Hill of Gold), on the shores of Lake Atitlan, near Volcanoes *Atitlan* and *Toliman*. It takes place some undetermined hundreds of years ago.

A great hunter here was admired by many and emulated by a particular young acquaintance. The young man asked the hunter if he could accompany him to the forested slopes and craters of the volcanoes to hunt and learn the other's secrets. The hunter agreed, under the condition that the aspirant was willing to hunt late at night. They left during daylight and moved uphill through the woods as it grew dark, toward one of the volcano craters. Upon reaching it, they rested for awhile in a small clearing. The time was approaching midnight.

On that hour, the hunter put on a spectacle that astonished his young ward. He first ceremoniously spit into the soil and, then, did three summersaults. Suddenly, he transformed into a lion. He then leaped from the clearing and disappeared into the foliage. Soon, the young man heard some thrashing and animal sounds at a distance. A short while later, the hunter came back dragging a young deer. Aware that the hunter had somehow acquired superhuman powers, the young man determined to stay with him to learn more of his secrets.

Each night, the hunter would repeat the first night's performance and bring back game to the site of his companion. It became the young man 's job to clean and preserve the meat. Then, it would be hauled to a village for sale. Over time, the novice observed some of the kills. Among the secrets he learned was that, in attacking the throat of large game and killing it, the hunter avoided swallowing the victim's blood. One day, however, while still in the form of the lion, the hunter erred and allowed some of his prey's blood to slip down his throat. Upon returning to his human form, he became somewhat moody but said nothing about the incident. Shortly later, the pair went to sleep. Upon awakening in the morning, the young man was surprised to find his companion still asleep under covers. After sometime he tried to awaken him with a call and, later, with some nudges. These efforts were to no avail.

Finally, in mid-morning, he pulled back his companion's covers only to recoil in horror upon seeing there, instead of the hunter, a huge man-size snake. On being revealed, the snake quickly slithered away into the forest. The young man sat on the ground for some time, shaken by what had occurred. He was alone. But he had not only learned the hunter's secrets but had discovered the consequences of drinking the fresh blood of one's prey. He took upon himself the teacher's role and became a hunter of great renown. The snake was never seen again but continued to live in the region of the volcano.

NOTE: This appendix was written in 1999. Time-related family data and circumstances extant at that time have since undergone some change.

APPENDIX 2
INDIGENOUS ART ON CANVAS

Mayan painting in the style alternately described as "naif", "primitivist", "popular" and "paisajismo" has gained international attention in recent years, through exhibits held in such places as the National Palace of Guatemala and in museums and galleries in Europe and the United States. This style was recently the subject of a comprehensive illustrated book on the subject, entitled *Arte Naif*, initially published by UNESCO and since reprinted, first, by BANCAFE, Grupo Financiero del Pais, and secondly by *Fundacion Paiz*, the latter being a bilingual edition.

The two principal "schools" of Mayan Painting are geographically identified as centered in the Lake Atitlan Basin and in the relatively nearby Central Highlands town of Camalapa. The Atitlan School is primarily represented by The Tz'utujil communities of Santiago Atitlan, San Pedro La Laguna, and San Juan La Laguna. Camalapa is a Kaqchikel community. While these two schools share common elements each has features considered unique.

The popular work of indigenous artists was accorded little artistic value before the twentieth century although it was incorporated to some extent (and for practical reasons) into architecture and play production as early as the Spanish colonial period.

Early "respectable" art treating indigenous subject matter, most notably "Indianismo" and "costumbrismo" was done by Ladino or foreign artists and portrayed native people and culture in romanticized or idealized forms. Public recognition of contemporary Mayan paintings as a legitimate art form did not begin to emerge until the 1930's. Public appreciation was nourished by the "Revolution of October" (1944-54)

An oil painting by Felipe Ujpan Mendoza of San Juan La Laguna entitled "Just One More." The scene is of a group of drunken celebraters at the conclusion of a traditional Mayan Feast Day.

and experienced another boost, beginning in 1985, with the process of political democratization and a growing recognition of the unique value of multi-ethnicity in Guatemalan culture.

The contemporary Mayan style most closely approximates the genre traditionally known in Western art as Primitivism. At the same time, in it's considerable variations, it incorporates significant elements of other art genres. Some Mayan artists have also borrowed from the range of other established techniques, with variable success.

Characteristic features of Mayan oils are found in subject matter and style. The most common subjects are landscapes and rural community settings. In the case of the latter, most popular are ceremonial scenes. The painting of portraits, while relatively uncommon in the early contemporary period, have also become popular over time. This is more the case among the Comalapa painters. Portraits are invariably of indigenous people, mostly in ceremonial dress. the

portrayal of social activity is more characteristically narrative or anecdotal than interpretive.

Historical events are rarely depicted, but the theme of Mayan traditions is dominant and, in this respect, the art preserves the history of customary Mayan life. It is rare to find evidence of modern commercial conveniences in Mayan paintings or to find evidence of other cultures (e.g., Ladino, Black, or European). Contemporary Mayan art gives the impression of being self-taught and ingenuous. In it's fundamental form, it is simple and uni-dimensional. Groups of human subjects are commonly painted with little differentiation in appearance between individuals.

The above painting "Susto del Eclipse" by San Juan painter Diego Isaias Hernandez, depicts a community frightened by the occurrence of an eclipse/

At the left, Angelina Quix Ixtamer discusses one of her paintings with a visitor. Angelina is one of only a handful of female indigenous oil painters to date who have had her works publicly exhibited.

Physical features are simplistic, with facial expressions relatively undifferentiated, and bodies anatomically stiff. Size and shape of features are sometimes distorted. These qualities, to some extent, reflect self-taught skills and an effort at self-control. However, the departure from realism is sometimes a reflection of a penchant for free expression. Because of the "wooden' quality of figures and actions portrayed, Mayan art is sometimes said to lack *pathos*.

Above and to the left are oils by two of the most renowned painters of San Pedro La Laguna. Above is by Mariano Gonzalez Chavajay and to the left by Pedro Rafael Gonzalez Chavajay. These artists are cousins and contemporaries.

According to Lucrecia Mendez de Penedo, a contributing writer to *Arte Naif*, paintings of the Camalapan school are distinguished by a bright variety of colors, emotive control, carefully calculated and symmetrical composition of elements, innocent and rustic scenery, and the domination of ritualistic and festive scenes. The paintings of Atitlan are distinguished thematically by a more dramatic sense of realism and a subtler use of light and shade to "create an atmosphere charged with mystery," especially when dealing with native rites. Traditionally, within the Atitlan school, human figures have been more characteristically portrayed with disproportionately elongated limbs and with facial expressions that are impenetrable or pained. Mendez notes, however, a recent trend away from this exaggerated form. There is also within the Atitlan School a small group of painters who have focused attention on the recent war violence experienced around the Lake.

The skill, and perhaps the talent, for painting on canvass has spread along family lines through generations of accomplished artists. This is consistent with the character of Mayan culture where knowledge and technique are taught with great patience through demonstration, practice, and repetition of technique – generally within an extended family. Thus, many of the notable contemporary artists of Santiago and San Pedro bear the same family names as the early pioneers in this art form. The pioneers at Atitlan were Juan Sisay in Santiago and Rafael Gonzalez y Gonzalez in San Pedro. Sisay had his life cut short by assassination but not before he taught his techniques to Manuel Reanda. Today in Santiago two Reandas are prominent among the third generation of *Arte Naif* painters.

In San Pedro La Laguna, several prominent artists bear the name Gonzalez. Still, the family succession dynamic is far from an exclusive formula for success, as some accomplished artists take on students for pay and other talented artists learn through their own experimentation. This is especially so in the case of San Juan La Laguna where some accomplished painters have apprenticed under San Pedro painters

while others are completely self-taught. This has been almost exclusively a male area of endeavor with the primary exception being where some artists have tutored their wives.

Today, some indigenous artists are moving away from the traditional characteristics of *Arte Naif*. For some artists it is an incremental process and for others it is a broader jump. Among the incrementalists are Emilio Gonzalez Morales from San Pedro and his brother Juan Fermin who have pioneered painting from the perspective of being above and below the subject painted. These are known, respectively, as the *Vista del Pajaro* (birds-eye view) and *Vista de la Hormiga* (view of the ant). Among the most notable of the more impressionistic painters are Samuel Cumes P'op of San Pedro La Laguna and Rene Dionisio Chavajay of Sta. Maria Visitation, a small village near Atitlan. P'op did most of his initial work in pencil but has since shifted to oils. His themes almost exclusively depict man's violence to man or to nature.

The above painting by Emilio Gonzalez Morales, entitled "Adoration of the Eclipse," is done from the perspective known as *vista de la hormiga."*

The painting to the right by Samuel Cumes P'op, entitled "Relationship," expresses the relationship of indigenous mankind and nature.

While this appendix is primarily devoted to indigenous art, it is appropriate to recognize the works of Juan Francisco Guzman, a local artist who is not Mayan but who is an Atitlan native and paints almost exclusively in themes depicting Mayan culture.

Above are pencil sketches by Samuel Cumes P'op. The drawing on the left, entitled *Guatemala Herida*, depicts Guatemala crippled by the 36 years of civil war recently concluded. The drawing on the right, entitled *Superpoblacion,* shows Mother Earth severely crippled by the effects of overpopulation.

This work, entitled *Fuga Sustancial*, (Substantial Flight) is by Juan Francisco Guzman

APPENDIX 3
MAYAN MUSIC & DANCE

Mayan music has maintained its essential spiritual character over the roughly 500 years since the conquest of the ancient Mayan civilization by the Spanish Empire. The indigenous music heard at Lake Atitlan and the instruments used to play it here are essentially the same as found in the rest of the contemporary Mayan world. The most common of the instruments are the drum, flute, chirimia, and the marimba. The first two can be traced back to ancient times, the other two arrived with the Spaniards.

The original purpose of Mayan music was purely ritualistic. Music served to appease and honor the gods, express gratitude for divine intervention, and to solicit favor. The subjects of these rituals changed with the imposition of Christianity beginning in the sixteenth century. Over time, other outside influences came to influence not only the inventory of the instruments used and materials used to fabricate them, but the range of occasions for their use as well. Most important to the continued ritual role of Mayan music has been the Christian institution of the *cofradia* as it was adapted to the evangelization of the Maya. *Cofradias* were established by the missionaries as lay brotherhoods dedicated to the veneration of specific saints. The *cofradia* has historically been the key human resource of local Catholic indigenous communities. Traditional Mayan music constitutes an essential part of virtually all of their ceremonies.

A good place to gain a basic understanding of Mayan music is the *Casa K'ojom Musica Maya*, a small museum located at the Centro Cultural La Azotea in

This oil painting by Felipe Ujpan Mendoza entitled "La Cofradia en San Juan La Laguna" depicts a drummer and chirimia player with the leaders of a local cofradia and their wives.

the town of Jocotenango, in the department de Sacatepequez. According to Samuel Franco Arce, the museum's founder and an expert on traditional Mayan music, knowledge of the history of this music comes largely from artifacts dating back to the Classic Period (A.D. 250 – 280).

Musical instruments and rituals in which they were employed are depicted in murals, in manuscripts, and on pottery. Instruments portrayed included rasps, drums, flutes, rattles, and trumpets made from natural materials. These materials included animal parts such as skins, shells, bones and antlers; tree gourds with seeds inside, clay and wood. From the earliest days, being a musician was an occupational specialty and one open only to men.

The forces of Christianity replaced Mayan rituals with ceremonies honoring Christ and the saints. These ceremonies would come to range in length from short sacramental events to festivals lasting several days. The Spanish brought not only European instruments but instruments from other cultures with which the Spanish Empire had been in contact. The marimba was an African instrument. The chirimia originated in the Arab world. The Spanish also introduced the first string instruments to the Americas.

This oil painting by Antonio Vasquez Yojcom entitled "Musicians in the Cofradia" depicts musicians playing a marimba, a drum, and a chirimia participating in a cofradia ceremony.

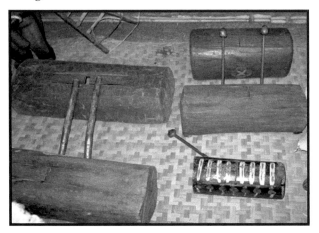

Above is a collection of slit log (*tun*) drums on display at the *Casa K'Ojom Musica Maya* Museum.

Drums are almost invariably present at Mayan rituals at Atitlan. Pre-Hispanic drums were of a variety of sizes, shapes and composition. According to Franco, all pre-Hispanic drums were beaten with the hand. Today, drums are beaten with sticks that have the contact ends covered in rubber. Most post-Conquest drums are cylindrical in shape with hide tops. An exception, rarely seen today but once common among the Atitlan Maya, is the tun. The tun drum is made by cutting slits into a hollow log in the form of an "H." This forms two vibrating tongues which enable the instrument to give off three distinct notes.

The flute and the chirimia, are woodwind instruments that are also part of most Mayan rituals at Atitlan. Of the two, the chirimia is the most popular here. It is also the more complex of the two in physical composition and the more difficult of the two instruments to play. The chirimia is made from cherry wood. The inside of the mouthpiece is formed by a dry palm leaf folded into a triangular shape and attached by a cord to a metal and wood casing. The mouthpiece must be damp to produce its characteristically sad sound.

Early Mayan flutes were made from a variety of materials, ranging from bone and pottery to jade. Flute music was considered divine. Most Mayan flutes are of the straight mouthpiece style although the transverse mouthpiece style was, in the past, quite common around Atitlan. Today, copies of the transverse style are commonly peddled as souvenirs in the streets of Panajachel and other tourist locations. Modern flutes are generally made of Carrizo cane or metal. They vary somewhat in size and shape.

The marimba is the national musical instrument of Guatemala. Marimbas are fabricated with a variety of different materials incorporating the basic components of a xylophone keyboard with resonators, played with sticks. The origin of this instrument is traced to Africa. The original Mayan marimba has gourd resonators and is similar to the type attributed originally to the African Bantu tribe. The gourds have openings at their bases which are surrounded with bees wax and covered with pig's intestine. The keyboard most commonly has 25 wooden keys which are struck by flexible wooden sticks with rubber coated ends. The modern marimba has largely

This oil painting, entitled "Rito de Agradecimiento" by Pedro Rafael Gonzalez Chavajay of San Pedro La Laguna, depicts four musicians playing at a Mayan rite of thanksgiving. Included are a chirimia player, a guitarist, and two drummers, one playing a slit log drum and the other playing the more common cylindrical shaped drum.

Dancing at annual feria in Solola (above and below.)
Photos Courtesy of Samuel R. Morgan.

Dancers in street parade during the annual feria
in San Juan La Laguna.

replaced the original Mayan marimba and is played for entertainment purposes at all kinds of civic and religious services.

Two other instruments brought by the Spaniards to the Americas and found at Atitlan are the guitar and the matraca. Dominican friars are credited with introducing the guitar here and incorporating it into church music. The matraca is a noisemaker, generally portable, made of hardwood and with a ratchet-type device on a handle that is rotated in a circular movement by hand. Large stationary versions are sometimes located on church top roofs near bell towers. According to Franco, the matraca's use is limited to the rituals of the Holy Week of Easter.

Visitors who come here expecting to hear melodious music coming from Mayan ensembles are likely to be disappointed. As Franco points out in his historical monograph on sale at the museum's gift store, there is a basic distinction between the function of indigenous Mayan music and European music "as an art." The function of Mayan music "... is not to evoke an aesthetic experience, but rather to arouse religious enthusiasm ... The Maya does not sing or dance to display his skill or his knowledge ... his music is the expression of his faith and hope and his fears for the Gods." Otherwise stated, this is simple music played with basic instruments to stimulate the primal regions of the mind. Hearing it ignites imagery of an ancient belief system with its core still intact.

Traditional Mayan music and dance have a complementary relationship that extends back to the Pre-conquest period. The evolution of dance however has followed a somewhat different trajectory than that of music. In the case of music, change has most notably been along the lines of an enrichment and sophistication of the inventory of instruments initially in use. In the case of dance, change has been more a conscious reshaping of the expression of spiritual beliefs, with the substitution of pre-Columbian themes with Christian ones and the large-scale introduction of European dance costumes to support these new themes of dance performance. Colorful costumes were also devised to depict Mayan nobility and warriors.

The most significant agents of change were missionaries who introduced Moorish dances and invented topical dances, sometimes imbedded with moral implications. The dance costumes were commonly of silk and velvet and decorated with colorful braid. Their general style was that of 16th century European finery. Masks were often made of faces with Western characteristics and painted white or red, often sporting golden hair. Among the most prevalent of the post-Conquest dances were the *Bailes* (dances) *del Torito, Los Mexicanos,* and *La Conquista.*

Among the most common of the few pre-Conquest dance themes that have survived, are the Deer Dance and the Snake Dance. The deer dance symbolizes the relationship between man and the deer and, more broadly, the struggle between mankind and animals. In its classic Mayan form, this dance is preceded by extensive preparations that include the careful selection of participants and the enactment of preliminary rituals accompanied by music and prayer. Costumed participants are dressed to represent a broad range of animals beside the deer, to include the monkey, tapir, and various wild cats.

While dance groups called *folklorico* commonly perform sophisticated, stylized dances with traditional Mayan themes of the pre-Conquest and colonial periods, the form of dancing most commonly done by contemporary Mayans during local *ferias* is much more basic and, indeed, little more than prancing during parades and shuffling and bumping around to the sound of the marimba or the music of the drum, flute, and *chirimia.*

APPENDIX 4
TALE OF THE XOCOMIL

You've already read about the climatic phenomenon called the *Xocomil*, the late morning wind that commonly agitates the Lake waters. As you might imagine, the Lake natives have at least one explanation for every natural thing they experience. This is one of these stories.

Once upon a time, when magic and the unexplainable lived in open harmony with the mundane, Lake Atitlan was a sleeping water without wind, clouds, or rain. The rain gods decided to tranform it into a vibrant, exciting place. One of these gods, Chac, decided to spark the process by sending the king of an anthill on a journey that would ultimately transform him, through an odyssey, into a Lake God who then would provide Atitlan with a dynamic personality.

Chac sent the ant king on a journey to the lakeshore to find water. It was such a tiring trip that when the ant arrived and began to take a drink, he fell into the Lake. As he sank, he saw a shiny crystal palace in the depths at a distance. When he reached the bottom he took refuge in a shell. For some reason he didn't drown. He admired the beauty of his surroundings but was saddened by the loss of his life above the surface. He cried and his tears turned into pearls.

It happened that the princess of the crystal palace played near his hiding place. She found some of the pearls and, then, found him. He explained his plight and asked her help. She promised to intercede in his behalf with her father who was king of the crystal palace and a magician.

When the king heard the story and saw the pearls he knew he was obliged to help the ant. He placed him in a fisherman's net, transformed him into a human baby, and caused the net to be quickly drawn to the surface. On the surface he was found by a fisherman amid a catch of fish. The fisherman brought him home, where he was raised by the fisherman and his wife, who until now, had been childless. They named him *Xocomil*.

As he grew, the boy realized he had magic powers but hid them from his parents. It reached a point, however, that he had to leave them for a new home at the summit of the volcano. There, he increasingly evolved into a godlike creature capable of changing form and agitating the Lake's water by whim. He would blow on its surface like a strong wind, from the top of the volcanoes. He would also tranform himself into a fishlike creature so that he could frolic in its depths with his old friends, the crystal palace king and the princess.

One night he met the moon goddess who crowned him with a crown of stars. Afterwards they lit up the sky above the volcanoes.

Some time later he gave up his human form altogether and became the spirit of Lake Atitlan. Since then, he has given the Lake its clouds, fog, storms, beautiful sky colors, and the high waters occasioned by his winds.

APPENDIX 5
THE MARRIAGE OF 2 FAITHS: EXEMPLIFIED IN JESUS CHRIST AND MAXIMON

Most of the Mayan people on the shores of Lake Atitlan are nominally Christian. But, their Christianity is meshed with a belief system that pre-dates the arrival of the Spanish. This earlier system served as the frame of reference for understanding the instructions of the missionaries and has continued to substantively influence the Mayan view of the Universe at Lake Atitlan.

This is specifically, the story of the evolution of the Tz'utujil faith system into the syncretic blend of religion that can still be experienced in Santiago Atitlan today. This account is largely indebted to the research of Vincent Stanzione, as published in his definitive work on the subject, *Rituals of Sacrifice.* Remember that Santiago Atitlan is essentially the population center of the Tz'utujil, one of two distinct Mayan groups that share the Atitlan Basin. The following belief is less strongly held and more intermixed with other ideas as one travels beyond this community's physical limits.

Let's begin with the origin of mankind. In the beginning, there was the "Old Couple", the first father and the first mother, who decided to create a small group of men and women (called *Nawales)* to serve as models for humanity. There were perhaps a dozen in all, "divinely" matched into husband-wife pairs. These were perfect people who loved to work and who worked hard. The men were primarily merchants who spent much of their time traveling. The women maintained the homes and dominated their small communities in the men's absence. The *Nawales* sensed they had a mission to help man rise above his animalistic nature which … "was constantly being tested by natural and supernatural forces."

They set the example and, "everything the *Nawales* did the people of Atitlan would come to imitate in order to become perfect models of the past…"

But, life was not perfect among this tight-knit group. The men began to have reason to fear that their wives would be unfaithful to them while they were traveling. So, they decided to carve a watchman out of a wood from a tree with magical properties, the *palo de pito.* The tree was asked if it was willing to accept the role of guardian of their woman and it acquiesced. They then set about to carve the tree into an image of the spirit God *Mam*, "the Ancient One, guardian of the people here on the face of the earth." With 40 axe hacks and 40 prayers, the essential work was done. Through this painful process, Mam was born in an earthly form. He was carved by the *Nawal* men and was dressed to perfection in the finest clothing by the *Nawal* women. The women then completed the job of giving him life by wrapping their head ribbons around his form and playing out songs of his spirit on a primitive marimba. This personification of *Mam* came to be known as *Maximon.*

Unfortunately *Maximon* was not quite up to his intended role. He began to seduce the wives of the absent men. When the men realized this, they decided they had to emasculate the figure that they had created. They cut off his arms and legs, and further dismembered the limbs at the various joints. They disfigured his face. When the surgery was over, Maximon had been deprived of all of his human potentials to include base human urges." He became the 'Lord' of all that was concerned with sexuality on the face of the earth and, from that day on, he stopped wasting energies on sexual pursuits. His very abstinence and celibacy gave him greater magical powers and, through the process of mentally working through his own dismemberment' he acquired magical power in putting "ill human beings back together again."

Stanzione explains that Maximon is but one manifestation of the great god Mam. One can draw a parallel between Him and Jesus, with the latter as the earthly manifestation of the Christian God. Indeed, the believers in Maximon see him somewhat as a brother of Christ who, like Christ, submitted himself to martyrdom for the sake of the renewal of humanity. This parallel role is played out with the icons of Christ and Maximon side by side, each year during Easter week.

Maximon is venerated by an indigenous Christian cult, a *cofradia*, affiliated with the Catholic Church. The *cofradia* maintains constant vigil over *Maximon's* statue which is kept on public display in periodically changing locations in town. *Maximon's* role and stature defy simple definition. The interpretation of his being and his significance varies even among the Tz'utujils. Among his most devout followers he is viewed at a level close to that of Christ, somewhat like his Mayan brother. More commonly he is viewed as a worldly saint who differs from the traditional Christian version in that he enjoys liquor and cigars. More important, he is accessible to those who seek God's acceptance (or even intercession in support) of human vice or frailties.

Many conservative Catholic and Evangelical Mayans see Maximon as an intrinsically evil figure, and a bane on respectable mainstream Christianity. One account holds that *Maximon* was "invented" in the Spanish colonial period by a physician, to help cure mental illness. Over time, *Maximon* has gained international tourist attention. The tourist literature commonly describes his complex *persona* as a composite of those of *San Simon* (Saint Simon), Judas Iscariot, the Mayan god, *Ry Laj Man*, and the Conquistador Pedro Alvarado.

Maximon as displayed in *cofradia* chapel in Santiago Atitlan.

Curandero Don Jose alongside image of Maximon maintained in his house at Cerro de Oro.

APPENDIX 6
MEDICINAL PLANTS OF THE LAKE BASIN

Besides cradling the most beautiful lake in the world, the Lake Atitlan Basin is a cornucopia of medicinal plants – many of which have been used by Mayan curanderos of the Lake since pre-Columbian times. The original inventory of medicinal plants was slim compared to what is grown here today. Many of these plants were brought to the Americas in the colonial period by the Spaniards. Others have been introduced relatively recently. But, regardless of how or when they arrived, a large variety of medicinal plants thrive effortlessly here today. Many of them even grow wild. And now, alongside the Mayan shaman, conventional healthcare practicioners and rural medicine clinics are exploiting the value of these plants for healing.

Armando Caceres in his book *Plantas de Uso Medicinal en Guatemala* (University of San Carlos Press, 2d ed., 1999), lists 120 plants of medicinal use found in Guatemala. The Mesoamerican Study Center for Appropriate Technology (CEMAT) in it's two-volume work *Fichas Populares Sobre Plantas Medicinales* identifies 65 medicinal plants that grow in the Lake Atitlan region. In my own herb garden at "Los Encuentros Posada y Centro Cultural" in Panajachel, I have planted 34 different medicinal plants (some of which are trees).

There are numerous *naturistas* and many others who cultivate their own medicinal herb gardens around the Lake. There are several pharmacies that sell locally produced medicinal herb products.

Andres Culum Matzar, from the lakeside community of San Pablo La Laguna, is one of the more

Boldo is a tree that thrives at high altitudes. It's leaves are primarily used to treat liver maladies.

Apazote is a plant whose flowers and leaves are used as both condiments and as medicinal herbs for treating liver problems, irregularities in menstrual flow, and in eliminating parasites.

visible *naturistas*. He has his own pharmacy in-town that sells products made of medicinal herbs. He has also worked with a Panajachel-based organization, *Tradiciones Mayas,* which teaches the art of growing and processing medicinal herbs to the populations of several small communities in the Lake vicinity. An organization at the Lake which plays a much larger role in exploiting the use of medicinal plants for healing is *Vivamos Mejor.* According to Rebecca Sanchez of that organization's Panajachel headquarters, *Vivamos Mejor* has six pharmacies which dispense products made of medicinal herbs and two sites where the cultivation and processing of medicinal herbs for self-use is taught. The pharmacies make use of 25 – 30 different medicinal plants in 23 products that range from shampoo and cough syrup to dried herbs for infusions (teas) and decoctions (cooked brews).

Some of these plants, like the Matasano tree, from whose Kaqchikel word the town of *Panachachel* is derived, are virtually unknown to North American and European medicinal plant users. Many visitors admire the beautiful lavender-colored flowers of the Jacaranda tree common here without realizing that the flowers and leaves provide a tea for the treatment of amoebas. Other plants like Echinacea and Valerian are much better known to foreign visitors.

The popularity of medicinal plants at the Lake is driven by both the cultural acceptance of this form of medicine and the economic reality that "hi-tech" conventional drugs are beyond the "pocketbook" of many. The popularity of this mode of treating sickness has quite different roots in the "developed" world familiar to most tourists. But, in both cases, medicinal plants have found a niche which offers a way to treat sickness other than the knee-jerk reliance on antibiotics which eventually leave both the budget and body bankrupt of alternatives to curing our illnesses.

The matasano (above) is a tree whose leaves, stems, fruit, and seeds are all used for a broad variety of ailments.

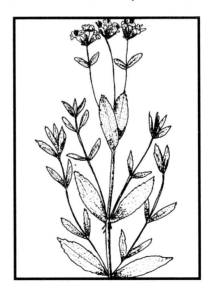

Pericon is a plant similar to St. John's Wort. Its flowers and leaves are used to treat anxiety, depression, and menstrual cramps.

APPENDIX 7
THE CATHOLIC TEMPLES OF THE LAKE BASIN

The first missionaries in Guatemala were Dominicans. Wandering members of this order began to Christianize Atitlan natives on the heels of the Spanish conquest of the area in 1524. However, the Dominicans built no churches at Atitlan.

In 1534, the Catholic Church established a religious administrative structure in Guatemala called a diocese. The diocese was divided into provinces which were further divided into parishes (variably called over time *doctrinas, curatos, or parroquias*). The Franciscan Order arrived in Guatemala in 1540, and was assigned the Lake region to missionize. By 1550 the Franciscans were well-established around Atitlan, although squabbling between the Franciscan and Dominican orders somewhat distracted from a focused missionary effort. The Franciscan strategy was to concentrate native populations in communities focused on Christian teaching and the support of the two new dominant institutions; the Catholic Church and the Spanish Crown.

These events roughly corresponded with the creation of a secular municipal-level administrative structure in Guatemala in the form of *corregimientos.* Two *corregimientos* were established at Atitlan; one based in Solola and the other in Santiago Atitlan. These places were officially founded *as pueblos* in 1547. Panajachel (initially known as *San Francisco de Panajachel*) was founded about the same time, under the administration of Solola. Lesser lakeside communities also placed under the *corregimiento* of Solola were San Jorge, Santa Cruz, and San Marcos.

By 1567, the Franciscans had undertaken the construction of three major churches in the Lake region; in Solola, Santiago Atitlan and Panajachel. They also began building places of worship elsewhere. Characteristically, all but the largest of the early churches were built of adobe, with straw roofs. Santiago was a province seat and the mission center (*cabecera de doctrina*) for ministering the Tz'utujil population. Solola was assigned the status of mission center for the Kaqchikel population. Solola's church, Our Lady of the Assumption, was to be the largest and most elaborate of all.

By Royal mandate, the building of mission churches was to be financed, in part, by the *corregimientos*. However, in many cases, this task was almost exclusively accomplished by the local native communities with their own resources. Construction was generally slow. For example, it was not until 1643 that a mission structure (a *convento*) was built to complement the church of Saint Francis of Assisi in Panajachel.

The Christianization of the Mayans was a formidable challenge undertaken with meager resources. It was carried out through a multifaceted methodology that incorporated winning the good will of indigenous leaders and capitalizing on the dynamics of the existing belief system. The strategy was largely one of finding parallels between fundamental Mayan beliefs and Christian beliefs and substituting Christian concepts and identities for those important in Mayan religion.

While Mayan religion at the time of the Conquest was polytheistic, it had, earlier, been based on the belief in an almighty god. The Carmelite, Jesus Maria Sarasa, In his work *Guatemala: Una Mision Carmelita*, describes Mayan religion as chronologically evolving from this earlier "pure" monotheistic stage to a stage characterized by a "plurality of gods and the offering of human sacrifices." Monotheism prevailed during the Classic Period of Mayan history. The change was sparked by a Toltec invasion of Mayan territory in the 9th century A.D. Toltec religion embraced the dualistic notion of the struggle between the forces of good and evil, personified in benevolent and evil gods, some of greater importance than others.

Religion played an important role in Native American society and was celebrated by the building of temples and monuments and the practice of a broad range of ceremonies incorporating dances, fiestas, magic rites, sacrifices, and the worship of icons.

Toward this end, the first thrust of Christian evangelization was directed toward establishing what Sarasa describes as the "external cult of God and the Saints," to include the ceremonies that surrounded these figures. Thus, Christian saints were substituted for gods and the practice of idolatry was channeled into associations dedicated to specific saints. One way or another, important Mayan rituals were translated into Catholic ones or otherwise subsumed into them. Where the dates of pagan festivals didn't practically fit this scheme, Christian ceremonies were instituted to replace these.

Church of St. Francis of Assisi, Panajachel

Old bell in detached belltower across the open churchground area in front of the church.

Church of Saint James the Apostle, Santiago Atitlan

According to Sarasa, a difficult task facing the missionaries was reorienting the Mayans to practice religion indoors, a matter important to Catholicism because of the traditional importance attached to a church as the center of worship. The first step was to establish a simple worship site at one corner of a field and, then, to add three others to form the four cardinal directions, while forming the symbol of a Christian cross. Next, a simple roofless church was built at the center. Afterwards, the structure was elaborated with a grass roof, wood support, and so on.

By 1567, church building had become considerably more sophisticated. The Franciscans had undertaken the construction of three major churches in the Lake region; in Solola, Santiago Atitlan and Panajachel. They also began building

places of worship in other communities around the Lake. Sarasa laments that, despite all the effort placed on the superficial traits of Christianity (e.g., temples, rituals, festivals, and the practice of baptism), insufficient energy was devoted to a patient, effective, and constant program of religious instruction. Consequently, pre-Columbian beliefs continued to co-exist and mix with Christian theology – producing beliefs and symbols coined "syncretic" by anthropologists. This synthesis was not an event that took place in a single point of time but, rather, was an ongoing one, with a life of its own.

Long after Christ's death on the cross and the subsequent religious evangelization of the Mayans by the Franciscan missionaries, the Tz'utjils in Santiago Atitlan instituted the Cofradia Santa Cruz, focused on Maximon, discussed in Appendix 5.

By 1690, Panajachel was a mission center with four visitas: Concepcion, San Andres, San Antonio and Sta. Catarina. San Antonio and Sta. Catarina were established lakeside; San Andres and Concepcion on the high ground above the Lake. The church built in Panajachel by the Franciscans was named in honor of their founder, St. Francis of Assisi. It's design is considered "Churrigueresque." Its unstuccoed façade of hewed stone block is among the most unique in Guatemala, with a multitude of statuary niches and a skyline that steps up from the sides to a squarish peak. Along the top are a series of quadrangular spikes.

Of the communities administered by Panajachel, Concepcion has the most physically impressive surviving colonial-era church. The church's size and sophistication presents a somewhat strangely out-of-place appearance today, as Concepcion has remained a remote, tiny farm village reached by a narrow, winding road from the city of Solola, which has only recently been paved. The church sits on a basic village square, looming over surrounding single—story structures.

The church of Concepcion's uniqueness merits a detailed description. It's exterior is stuccoed; with very elaborate designs in the façade. The façade has two tiers with altar niches. The niches on the first level are empty. Those on the second level have small masonry statues. A third tier incorporates a single, centered belfry which holds one large bell (dated 1621) and two smaller bells. The façade is further adorned by two crowned lions. Above the portal is inscribed the date 1621 and words in old Latin, translated by an anonymous friar for the local municipal records as "Finished in honor of the Blessed Virgin Maria by King Felipe IV." The year 1621 was the first of this king's reign, which ended in 1665. The façade's skyline is characterized by a series of spiked quadrangles with miniatures of simple, domed chapels at each end. The church's interior has a single nave. The ceiling is peaked and made of plain wooden planking, reinforced with elaborately carved wood pieces that cross over the ceiling and run along its two sides where the ceiling meets the walls. The interior is dominated by a gilded, decoratively carved, multi-tiered retablo mayor that contains six statuary niches and several oil paintings. A figure of Mary in the persona of the "Immaculate Conception" is centered on the first tier and dominates the retablo. The interior also holds two gilded side retablos with statuary and some lesser side altars.

Church of the Immaculate Conception, Concepción

Bells in church belfry, tied with leather straps to a support beam.

A HONRA DXI SSª AC NIO ͼ SΦ·ḤḤIPḤ·NRINAͱ ·1621

The above caption over the church main portal announces the date of the church's inauguration.

Church of St. Catherine, Sta. Catarina Palopó

These bells are in a detached bell tower across the front open area of the churchgrounds.

Church of St. Anthony of Padua, San Antonio Palopó

These bells are in a detached bell tower alongside the front of the church.

Church of St. Luke, San Lucas Toliman

Baptismal font inside side chapel of Church of St. Luke.

The Church of St. Peter, San Pedro La Laguna (Destroyed)

Church of St. John the Baptist, San Juan La Laguna

Wood columns supporting roof of administrative building attached to church. Each is unique in carving detail.

Church of St. Paul, San Pablo La Laguna

Church of St. Helena of the Cross, Santa Cruz La Laguna

Church of St. George, San Jorge La Laguna

The challenges of establishing and maintaining substantial structures as temples of worship were in all cases formidable around the Lake. The fate that would befall the church of Solola, the most important of all of these temples, is illustrative of this point. The first structure, of adobe, was damaged by an earthquake shortly after its completion in 1566. A larger structure was essentially completed in 1584, but was badly damaged that year by a lightning strike. It was repaired and over time elaborated. But, in 1773 the entire structure was reduced to rubble by an earthquake. In took until 1781 to rebuild a provisional church, but it was only of mud and straw. It, at any rate, was destroyed by fire three years later. The construction of another church was undertaken but it was destroyed, still unfinished, by an earthquake in 1862. Whatever reconstruction may have been resumed was undone by still another earthquake in 1902. Further repetitive earthquakes forestalled any further effort to undertake new construction until 1941. The current cathedral was started shortly afterward and was not completed until 1978.

Panajachel's Church of San Francisco also suffered heavily over time, although it is believed that the church that stands today is essentially the original temple. The available historical record is sketchy. There are no clues in the parish archives. Handwritten records of the church's *Cofradia de San Francisco* say that the church was destroyed in 1716 and rebuilt between 1958 – 1962 by a priest named Juan Manuel. This leaves a lot unaccounted for. Robert Hinshaw's *Panajachel: A Guatemalan town in 30-Year Perspective*, infers the church had a roof before "… the 1903 earthquake that toppled virtually every church in the region." This is the same earthquake elsewhere recorded as having occurred in 1902. Hinshaw also reports that Panajachel did not have a Catholic priest between 1903 and 1952.

Tax (1951) refers to the Panajachel colonial church of the 1940's as a ruin. Local residents have recounted to me that the church of the 1950's, while in use, lacked intact side walls and, except for the sanctuary, most of it's roof.

A long-time resident of the period verified Rev. Juan Manuel's key role in the church's restoration. He is remembered as a dynamic, energetic priest who dressed in "street" clothes rather than clerical habit. Sarasa's book (1991) provides useful insight on some key events which impacted on all of the churches in the Lake region in the 19th and 20th century as well some specifics on Rev. Juan Manuel.

Sarasa notes that earthquakes of 1862, 1902, 1942 and 1976 were especially damaging to churches. Fires, and floods also took a toll on some. The goals of maintaining and improving church property in the 19th century were complicated by the rise of the first of the Liberal regimes to national power, beginning in 1831. Liberal governments generally sought to reduce the power of traditional conservative institutions like the Catholic Church. Under the presidency of Justo Rufino Barrios, beginning in 1870, laws were passed limiting church influence, expropriating church property, and expelling and restricting the entry of foreign clerics. The latter development impacted especially hard in areas like the Lake region, as the Catholic Church had never been very successful in recruiting clergy from the indigenous sector. Most Guatemalan priests were Ladino and the smaller total number of priests now available were mostly posted to serve urban areas of greater population concentration.

Sarasa describes the outcome of the above circumstances and the role played here by the Carmelite Order of Spain following their arrival at Atitlan in 1954. The Carmelites were assigned the bulk of the parishes of the Lake Basin. Sarasa reports that, at that time, all of the churches of the Lake were in a bad state of physical decomposition. The task of renovating church property, however, was somewhat facilitated at that point by the fall of the Arbenz government and the ascendancy to the presidency of Castillo Armas, who came to be considered as "the restorer of the rights of the Church." Juan Manuel Amezaga is listed as the second Carmelite *Religioso* assigned to Panajachel. He is subsequently listed as one of three who had "abandoned the order" by virtue of having been secularized.

Beyond natural and political events, the fates of the various community churches of the early Spanish period were influenced by the social and economic evolution of the communities they served. San Andres Semetabaj is alongside the main road that runs the Lake's rim on the north side. This community has experienced modest growth and modernization over time and has lost much of it's early Mayan character. Its old church is a badly deteriorated ruin, although the surviving façade still provides evidence of an earlier elegance. San Antonio Palopo and Sta. Catarina Palopo have remained very traditional communities and their colonial-era churches have survived intact. The church of Sta. Catarina, named after St. Catherine of Alexandria, is relatively simple and sparcely appointed. Perhaps its most important relic is the church tower bell which carries the date 1762. In contrast, the colonial church of San Antonio Palopo has an impressively elaborate interior, complete with a large gilded *retablo mayor* (main altar backdrop) and a good collection of impressive old statuary.

On the Lake's southern shores, the *cabecera* of Santiago initially administered to three *pueblos* in the same general time frame; San Lucas, San Pedro, and San Pablo. The mission of Santiago was located and architecturally constructed to make a strong statement of strength and authority. The complex resides above its own plaza, above the town market place. It is a large fortress-style structure.

The church interior holds a variety of interesting objects to include wood furnishings skillfully carved with images of Christian and pre-Columbian Mayan religious character intermingled in an expression of religious syncretism. The interior holds a large array of statues with European facial features, outfitted in indigenous dress.

One variation of the escutcheon Of the Franciscan order. The essential elements are a bared arm and a sleeved arm nailed to a cross. This escutcheon is located above the main portal of the Solola cathedral.

San Lucas, the largest of the three early *visitas* of Santiago, has a large colonial-era church, probably 17th Century, with marked similarities to the church of Concepcion, although it is smaller. The church has a variety of interesting statuary inside, some of which probably date back to the church's founding. Interestingly, the church of San Lucas is considerably distant from the town's current main square. The explanation is that the original town square was destroyed by fire and relocated when rebuilt.

San Pedro, while initially a *visita* of Santiago, later became a *parroquia*, administering the *visitas* of San Juan, San Pablo, San Marcos, and two villages further removed from the Lake, Sta. Clara, and La Visitacion. Its first substantial church was built in the 17th century. This temple continued to be improved until it was largely destroyed by fire in the 19th century. It's *coup de grace* was administered by the earthquake of 1902. San Pedro's current church is not especially noteworthy in construction or appearance.

San Juan La Laguna was founded as a pueblo between 1618 and 1623. It has a colonial-era church that has witnessed at least two major reconstructions. It was largely destroyed by fire in 1819, rebuilt, and destroyed again by the earthquake of 1902. Still, the church has managed to retain some of its original charm and is cherished by its congregation as the original temple.

The original colonial church constructed in San Pablo in the 17th century was very similar in size and appearance to San Pedro's early church, a somewhat remarkable fact in view of San Pablo's smaller size and lesser status. This church suffered from repeated earthquakes and was badly damaged by fire during an annual celebration of its patron saint. It was restored in 1821 but totally destroyed, except for its foundation and façade, by the earthquake of 1902. Today's church is colonial in appearance and apparently built on the foundation of the original church.

The lakeside communities of San Marcos and Santa Cruz La Laguna were also founded in the 16th century as pueblos under the administration of the *corregimiento* of Solola. However, the repeated relocations of San Marcos had the net effect of placing it further to the west than originally and further from the direct influence of Solola. These relocations also hindered the construction of a substantial church. It was known to have a church in 1725 built of adobe, with a straw roof. It is recorded that the church that stood in 1798 was totally destroyed that year by a fire which also destroyed all its contents. Another church was built but it was destroyed by an earthquake in 1827. It was rebuilt but, like those in neighboring San Juan and San Pablo, it was destroyed again, by the earthquake of 1902. San Marcos now has an attractive new church built out of local fieldstone.

Sta. Cruz la Laguna has conserved its colonial-era church, which the residents believe is the original 16th century temple. Considering the community's uphill move from its original shoreline site, the church is more likely late 17th century. This church is dedicated to Santa Helena of the Cross, the town's patroness. The church's size and simple white-washed stucco face is along the style of the churches of Sta. Catarina and San Jorge. The interior is spartanly furnished. The altar is a modern, plaster-faced object, probably built of block. The church has a relatively new plank wood ceiling that conceals a contemporary laminate roof. The interior walls are unadorned, without niches. The statuary is exposed carved wood, generally primitive in style and weather worn. Some of it is colonial-era

Church of St. Andrew, San Andres Semetebaj

This church is in the process of being restored. Above is how it appeared before 1999; below in 2002.

and probably quite valuable. The figures are simply lined-up against the walls.

San Jorge was a *visita* of Solola, originally located on the lakeshore. In the mid-17th century, the village was destroyed by flood and relocated uphill. San Jorge holds a small but picturesque colonial-era church with a sizable assortment of old statuary, colorfully dressed in clothing of native design, most certainly from the original church.

In 1753, the doctrinas around the Lake were taken away from the missionary orders and placed directly under diocesan administration. Diocesan priests began to administer to congregations, although missionaries continued to serve in some parishes. As already mentioned, the Church lost its capacity to staff these churches between the mid-19th and mid 20th centuries. This situation has since changed and missionaries are again playing an important role in religious life at the Lake, with the Carmelite Order being the most prevalent.

INTERIOR CHURCH DESIGN

The interior designs of Atitlan colonial-era churches are relatively simple. For the most part, the public-access area is a single hall with a main aisle (nave), there are no transepts or side chapels other than an occasional isolated baptismal area.

Most of the naves are small and rectangular, with plastered walls and flat wooden ceilings. The ceilings are constructed of wood beams and planking. Most of the walls are flat and devoid of decorative effects. Most of the ceiling woodwork is simple in shape and relatively free of decorative carving and painting.

Nave of the church of St. Francis of Assisi in Panajachel

Much of the decorative effect inside the church is achieved with cloth draped from ceilings to walls. Few of the church ceilings have domes. Where they exist, they are simply adorned.

Embellishments are largely limited to the larger churches, most notably the churches of Panajachel, Santiago, San Lucas, and Concepcion. A notable exception is the the sophisticated interior of the little church of San Antonio Palopo.

Ceiling of the Church of the Immaculate Conception, Town of Concepcion.

SANCTUARIES AND ALTARS

The main altar of a church is located in its sanctuary. Secondary altars are sometimes found along side walls or in side chapels. The decorative architectural support or screen behind an altar, called a *retablo*, is commonly decorated with religious objects and images in the forms of paintings, pictures, and statuary.

For the majority of the Lake's colonial-era churches, the only substantive *retablos* are those located behind the main altars. These are mostly simple structures or cloth screens crowned with a representation of the church's patron saint and embellished with a few other objects.

Main altar and *retablo mayor* of Church of Saint Anthony of Padua, San Antonio Palopo.

Main altar area of Church of Sta. Helena of the Cross, Santa Cruz La Laguna.

CHURCH STATUARY

The diverse character of the statuary found in the Lake's old churches ranges from colonial-era to new, from primitive to sophisticated, and from well preserved to weather-worn and damaged.

Much of it is found, as in any Catholic church throughout the world, garbed in traditional early-Christian period dress and located on pedestals or in wall niches. However, in many churches, some or most of the figures are at least sometimes clothed in Mayan costumes. This is more commonly the case in churches where the Mayan segment of the congregation has been afforded empowerment.

In many churches much of the statuary is simply leaned against an interior wall. To some extent this can be attributed to the mobile nature of the icons and their use in processions and other ceremonies outside of the church. However, much of the damaged old statuary along walls came from destroyed churches and has been relocated to replacement temples which have no design features for a fitting display of these relics.

Main altar and *retablo mayor* of the Church of the Immaculate Conception, town of Concepcion.

The above left statuary is from the Church of St. Catherine, Sta. Catarina Palopo.

Statuary at above right is from the Church of the Immaculate Conception, Concepcion.

Statuary at right is from Church of St. George, San Jorge La Laguna.

Statuary at left and below is from the Church of St. James, Santiago Atitlan.

APPENDIX 8
PRESERVING THE LAKE BASIN AS A BIOSYSTEM

As man increases his presence at Lake Atitlan and as modern culture increasingly imposes its influence here, the balance of nature becomes increasingly prone to destabilization. In that the value of the Lake to man depends on its survival as a living natural system, the challenge becomes one of adapting this system and man to each other's purposes. The challenge is exacerbated by unique demographic factors as well as the attractiveness of the Lake as a tourist destination.

Environmentally sensitive visitors are often surprised and bothered by the amount of visible garbage scattered about the landscape. Even more dangerous to the Lake's life are forms of contamination that don't meet the eye. Government and society had a somewhat "sleepy" start in addressing the potential seriousness of the problem. This can be attributed to a number of factors to include: the relative remoteness of the Lake, chronocially barrel-visioned, highly centralized national government, and a false sense of security generated by the reality of a relatively small rural population drawing off an immense lake with a huge volume of water.

However, the alarm has been sounded. Today, there are several organizational actors which play active roles in preserving the Lake as a healthy living entity. These include international and national environmentally-focused groups as well as local ones directly engaged in the dynamics of the Lake on a daily basis. In most cases, these groups work in collaboration, within their charters, to provide and apply resources to programs and projects that are defined through interaction at various levels. Historically, national and state-level governments have played a woefully small role in this effort, however, government involvement in this field has increased significantly in recent years. And, there is a good deal of catching up" to do.

The most important national governmental organization focused on the Lake environment is the Authority for the Sustainable Management of the Lake Atitlan Basin (AMSCLAE). The most visible of the non-governmental lake-wide groups is *Amigos del Lago*. The lakeside communities as well, through the initiative of municipal governments and private citizens, have formed committees to deal with local problems of environmental contamination, garbage collection and recycling, and environmental education.

AMSCLAE was formed in 1998 with the objectives of consolidating existing environmentally involved organizational structures and initiating programs in the areas of environmental education, waste management, and environmental policy. The overarching stated goal was the recovery and sustainment of the environmental quality of the Lake Atitlan basin to meet an increasing human demand. Toward this end, AMSCLAE created and manages specific programs in environmental policy and planning, environmental education, ecological and social studies, waste management, contamination control, forest and water management , and the management of water life resources. These programs are coordinated by an executive director and a board of representatives from six national level government agencies besides AMSCLAE, the national chamber of Tourism (CAMTUR), the Solola governor's office, and the municipal governments of 15 communities in the Lake basin. Among the accomplishments of this organization in its short life to date are: the implementation of an impressive public environmental educational program through a wide range of venues; the establishment of municipal garbage treatment centers and landfills; the clean-up of unauthorized dump sites; the establishment and support of a network of refuse recycle sites and collection sites for hazardous contaminants; the planning for and installation of septic and drainage systems in several communities; the rehabilitation of existing waste treatment plants and the planning for additional plants; and the organization, material support of, and participation in large-scale, area garbage cleanups.

The *Asociacion de Amigos del Lago,* was formed in 1990, well before the establishment of AMSCLAE, mostly by lakeside landowners who had become concerned about the effects of increasing man-induced pollution and the lack of an effective government program to deal with it. The character of its membership has diversified over time. An important challenge undertaken by the Association has been mobilizing the Lake Basin's population to reverse harmful practices that have increasingly tended to contaminate the Lake. The immensity of this challenge resides in fundamental cultural differences and racial antagonism between a small white elite and an historically exploited Mayan majority. There is little

basis for trust between the two sectors. But the imperative to save the Lake is a strong reason to place differences aside and work toward a common cause.

The *Amigos del Lago* plays both a "concerned citizen" role in monitoring government environmental actions and an activist role in attacking problems within its capabilities. It shares environmental concerns for the Lake with AMSCLAE and other public and private parties. With a core membership with substantial business contacts and enough resources to sustain a baseline operating budget, *Amigos del Lago* has fielded an assortment of programs tied to a strategy that stresses the importance of environmental education across generational lines and the need for cooperation at all levels of society.

With a limited budget, and working in a grossly under-funded area of public need, it conducts an active promotional campaign to expand membership and to obtain more resources for established programs. While it can't fund costly waste treatment and garbage collection systems needed at Atitlan, it coaxes and coordinates a range of resources outside of its direct control to work to reduce environmental contamination. Among its initiatives is the periodic conduct of lake-wide garbage cleanups in collaboration with Atitlan communities and supported by governmental agencies and private organizations. These projects include both the collection of large quantities of garbage from the Lake basin and the evacuation of it to a Guatemala City garbage dump.

The challenge of educating the Mayan population of the Lake about the dangers of modern contaminants is formidable. The future lies in the education of the children. But, the effectiveness of this education depends on a broader appreciation of the effort by adult generations. There is nothing in Mayan history that has prepared these people for problems associated with containers which don't decompose naturally. Nor, is there anything in their cultural heritage that creates an appreciation for the toxicity of man-made chemical products and pollution caused by the gasoline engine. The profit sector of modern mass culture has loaded the environment with products to promote material progress without a conscience for dealing with the side effects. Adult generations of Mayans are just beginning to appreciate the consequences.

The Amigos del Lago operates an environmental education program with 52 pilot schools that reaches approximately 11,000 students yearly. The organization hires *capacitadores* (facilitators) who help teachers prepare instruction and activities which support monthly environmental themes. An important tool for this project is an annual calendar produced by the *Amigos* which is illustrated by art works created by children, selected through an annual art competition that focuses environmental themes. The Amigos have also conducted a vacation program that exposes children to activities such as plant cultivation and reforestation. A new project has involved the recycling of plastic containers by compacting them into wall building material that is used in local construction. The plastic materials are largely collected in community school centers.

As one might expect, the effectiveness of local committees vary somewhat from community to community. Panajachel's *Comite Pro Sanamiento Ambiental* is an especially active association of private citizens which draws on support from the municipal government, the above mentioned organizations, and other outside resources when available. Such "Grass Roots" organizations provide the critical human resources that, in the final analysis, will play the key role in gaining the long-term local support critical to reducing environmental pollution.

SOURCES:

Aguirre, P. Gerardo P., OCD. 1972. *La Cruz de Nimajuyu: Historia de la Parroquia de San Pedro La Laguna.* Guatemala.

Batz, Luis Raymundo. Undated. "Monografía Del Pueblo." (San Pedro La Laguna).

Bauer, Angelika. 1993. *Xocomil.* Guatemala: Litografias Modernas.

Brosnahan, Tom & Nancy Keller. 1997. *Guatemala, Belize & Yucatan.* Australia: Lonely Planet Publications.

Cáceres, Armando. 1999. *Plantas de Uso Medicinal en Guatemala.* Guatemala: Editorial Universitaria, Colección Monografias, Vol. No. 1, Guatemala, Universidad de San Carlos de Guatemala.

Características de la Población y de los Locales de Habitación Censados. 2003. República de Guatemala Instituto Nacional de Estadística Censos Nacionales XI de Población y VI de Habitación 2002.

Castellanos, Edwin J., Maricruz de Mejia, Beatriz Lopez, Nancy Giron and Willy Knedel. 1996. "Challenges of Data Integration in the Study of a Complex System: A Case Study of Lake Atitlan in Guatemala." Guatemala, Universidad de Valle de Guatemala and Medical Entemology Research and Training Unit/Guatemala-CDC..

Cattelan, Marino. 2001. *Guatemalan Mountains.* Guatemala: Xibalba Publications.

DePaz J., Christian. 1997. *Atitlan, Los Pueblos y El Lago.* Guatemala: Editorial Los Gemelos.

CEMAT and Laboratorio y Drogueria de Productos Fitofarmacéuticos FARMATA, S.A. 1996. *Fichas Populares Sobre Plantas Medicinales.* 2 Vols. Guatemala.

Cofiño de Prera, Lucrecia and Delia Quiñónez, eds. 1999. *Arte Naif: Guatemala,* Versión Abreviada, Guatemala, BANCAFE, Grupo Financiero del País. De la Sociedad de Geográfica y Historia de Guatemala.

Gall, Francis E., ed. 1980. *Diccionario Geográfico de Guatemala.* Guatemala: Instituto Geográfico Nacional, C.A.

Glassman, Paul. 1981. *Guatemala Guide.* New York: Passport Press.

INGUAT Brochure. Undated, *Atitlán.* Guatemala.

INGUAT Brochure. Undated. *Santiago Atitlán, Sololá.* Guatemala.

FUNDESA Magazine. 1997. *Destination Guatemala.* Guatemala.

Hinshaw, Robert E. 1975. *Panajachel: A Guatemalan Town in Thirty-Year Perspective.* Pittsburgh, Pennsylvania: University of Pittsburgh Press.

Mahler, Richard. 1993. *Guatemala: A Natural Destination.* Santa Fe, New Mexico: John Muir Publications.

McBride, Felix Webster.1943. *Cultural and Historical Geography of Southwest Guatemala.* Smithsonian Institution Institute of Social Anthropology, Publication No. 4. Washington, D.C.

Newhall, Christopher G. 1986. "Geology of the Lake Atitlan Region, Western Guatemala", Monograph, Doc 0579A,1/14/86 Rev. Draft. Hanover, New Hampshire: Dartmouth College.

Newhall, C.G. et al. 1986. "Recent Geologic History of Lake Atitlan, ACaldera Lake in Western Guatemala." Monograph.Wang Doc 4436B. 1/14/86 Rev., Hanover New Hampshire: Dartmouth College.

Newhall C.G. and Dzurisin. 1988. "Historical Unrest at Large Calderas of the World" USGS Bulletin 1855.

Orellana, Sandra. *The Tzutujil Mayas; Continuity and Change, 1250 – 1630.* Norman: University of Oklahoma Press.

Prahl Redondo, Carlos E. 1990. *Guia de Los Volcanes de Guatemala,* Guatemala: Club Andino Guatemalteco.

Petrich, Perla. Ed. 1998. *Pueblos y Santos del Lago Atitlán,* Guatemala: Casa de Estudios de Los Pueblos del Lago Atitlán.

———————- . 1999. *Historias, Historia del Lago Atitlán,* Guatemala, Casa de Estudios de Los Pueblos del Lago Atitlán.

Recinos, Adrian, Delia Goetz, and Dionosio Jose Chonay, trans. 1953. *The Annals of the Cakchiquels.* Norman: University of Oklahoma Press.

San Buenaventura de Atitlan Brochures, undated. "Guía del Lago de Atitlán, La Historia", and "Horse Trail & Nature Trail." Guatemala.

Sarasa, Jesús María. Undated. *Guatemala: Una Misión Carmelita. Padres Carmelitas,* Provincia San Joaquín de Navarra. Ediciones San Pablo.

Saravia, Albertina E. 1977. *Popol Wuh.* Guatemala: Editorial Piedra Santa.

Stanzione, Vincent. 2000. *Rituals of Sacrifice,* Guatemala: author published.

Tax, Sol. 1964. *El Capitalismo del Centavo: Una Economía Indígena de Guatemala.* Guatemala: Ministerio Público de Educación, Guatemala.

Whatmore, Mark & Peter Etringham. 1992. *The Real Guide: Guatemala and Belize.* New York: Prentice Hall Travel.